SUMMIT TALES

GRAEME POLE

SUMMIT TALES

Early Adventures in
the Canadian Rockies

Altitude Publishing

"Even where all men go, none may have stopped; what all men have seen, none may have observed."

James D. Forbes, 1842

"... Have no Doubt you will find this a very interesting country to go to as the mountains are very high and craggy [and] the whole country is very Rough and the weather in July will freeze a kyote so i am sure you will call it Grand."

Letter from outfitter Fred Stephens to American mountaineer Walter Wilcox, December 31, 1902

Cover: The collective knowledge of several well-travelled, modern mountaineers has failed to place the location of this image, which shows J. Norman Collie's party approaching a summit, probably in 1902.

Frontispiece: The Ramparts: Bastion Peak, Turret Mountain, and Mount Geike (l-r), from Tonquin Creek; Cyril G. Wates photographer

Opposite: The first ascent party on the summit of South Twin, 1924. W.O. Field photographer

Back Cover: The east face of Mt. Robson, showing the icy slope of the Kain Face that leads to the southeast ridge. Byron Harmon photographer, 1911

Publication Information

Canadian Cataloguing in Publication Data
Pole, Graeme, 1956-
 Summit tales / Graeme Pole.
Includes bibliographical references.
ISBN 1-55153-937-3
 1. Rocky Mountains, Canadian (B.C. and Alta.)--Biography. 2. Mountaineers--Rocky Mountains, Canadian (B.C. and Alta.)--History. I. Title.
FC218.A1P64 2005   796.522'092'2   C2005-900661-7

Design / Layout: Bryan Pezzi
Editor: Sebastian Hutchings

We acknowledge the financial support of the Government of Canada through the Book Publishing Industry Development Program (BPIDP) for our publishing activities.

Made in Western Canada
Printed and bound in Canada
by Friesens Printers, Altona, Manitoba

Altitude GreenTree Program
Altitude Publishing will plant in Canada twice as many trees as were used in the manufacturing of this book.

9 8 7 6 5 4 3 2 1

Altitude Publishing Canada Ltd.
1500 Railway Avenue
Canmore, Alberta
Canada T1W 1P6

Contents

Prologue

A ugust 29, 1897, was a banner day for mountaineering in the Rockies. The party had started late for the peak. Now, in the building heat of late morning, John Norman Collie, George Baker, and their Swiss guide, Peter Sarbach, toiled across the glacier. Sarbach grunted under the load of heavy equipment that Baker used to survey and to photograph the Rockies.

An icefall separated the lower glacier from the final approach to Mt. Freshfield. The trio skirted the chaos of ice by climbing a cliff. From the upper glacier, Sarbach chopped steps in an icy slope, leading his party to the southeast ridge, where the summit loomed close and easy to reach.

Collie, who had been promoting haste down below, now saw that the ridgecrest offered Baker a splendid panorama of the surrounding mountains. He encouraged his colleague to set up the equipment while he nipped around a rock rib and across a snow-slope to have a look at the unknown

Opposite: W.O. Field's party approaches the summit of Epaulette Mountain in 1924.

country to the north. Sarbach, thinking that the surveying would occupy a short interval before the party renewed its attempt, took a nap.

Collie would later describe those moments high on Mt. Freshfield: "There is a great, if undefinable, pleasure in standing on a high mountain summit in a country but imperfectly known; so many uncertainties vanish in a moment, often with the comment – spoken or unspoken – 'I thought so'; while a host of new possibilities and further queries take their place."

By the time Baker completed the survey work and Sarbach awoke, it was late afternoon. The party faced a long descent to camp. To go for the peak would have meant a night on the mountain with minimal gear. Collie and Baker gladly turned their backs on the untrodden summit. Sarbach was scandalized. To him, the peak would have been another feather in his cap. But this was not Switzerland. These clients in Canada were different. To most of them, climbing a mountain mattered less than the adventure of getting there, and mapping the surrounding country for future possibilities.

Forty-Three Mountains and Three Hundred Photographs

To the Siksika (Blackfoot) Nation, they are The Backbone of the World. The first fur trade voyageurs who saw them, shimmering, snow-clad on the western skyline, called them Les Montagnes des Pierres Brilliantes – The Mountains of Brilliant Stones. The English-speaking fur trade partners of the North West Company altered the metaphor – the distant crags became The Shining Mountains. When European and Canadian explorers finally tackled the peaks head-on, and their boots and moccasins bumped against unyielding stone, something of the poetry went out of the description. The name that would stick was a banal description of the continent's most impressive limestone barrier – the Rocky Mountains.

The earliest climbs in the Canadian Rockies took place in a time beyond written history, when First Nations warriors made spirit quests, or pursued bighorn sheep and mountain goats summitward. Europeans and Canadians made their first climbs as the fur trade moved west. Peter Fidler, a surveyor for the Hudson's Bay Company, ascended Thunder Mountain in the southern

---

Opposite: "Two persons alone can conduct the camera and the instrumental work at a [camera] station, and one may be a porter to help carry the instruments. It is better to have three in case of an accident and to accelerate operations." J.J. McArthur leads and W.S. Drewry follows in this staged view showing surveyors in action, ca. 1891.

Above: J.J. McArthur took this view of the north glacier of Mt. Hector in 1887 from the summit now known as Mt. Andromache. The climbing guidebook to the southern Rockies lists the first ascent of Mt. Andromache as having been made in 1948.

Rockies in 1792. A year later, Alexander Mackenzie hiked up an unnamed summit alongside his namesake river. At the top, he discovered an abandoned First Nation camp. "We were obliged to shorten our stay here," he later wrote, "on account of the swarms of muskettoes [mosquitoes] that attacked us and were the only inhabitants of the place."

Above: W.S. Drewry took this panoramic photograph on the summit of "Signal 18" in 1890. The mountain is now called Mt. McArthur. Views such as this are a remarkable benchmark against which to measure changes in glaciation. The President is the prominent mountain in the centre.

Left: Some assembly required: surveyors used a photo-theodolite, such as this model made in France, to measure horizontal and vertical angles. But first they had to pack the device to a camera station and assemble it.

David Thompson, Duncan McGillivray, and a companion working for the North West Company, climbed a mountain near present-day Exshaw in 1800. It was the last day of November, so the party did not have to contend with mosquitoes. In a journal entry, Thompson rhapsodized on the scene: "Our view from the heights and eastward was vast & unbounded – the eye had not strength to discriminate its termination: to the westward hills & rocks rose to our view covered with snow, here rising, there subsiding, but their tops nearly of an equal height every where. Never before did I behold so just, so perfect a resemblance to the waves of the ocean in the wintry storm."

In making each of these ascents, the fur traders became incidental mountaineers, yet remained more

intent on surveying the country than on seeking the challenge of a climb. David Douglas was the first "recreational" mountaineer in the Rockies and in Canada. On May 1, 1827, prompted by no other calling than to achieve the summit, he sauntered up a lowly peak near Athabasca Pass in what is now Jasper National Park. As the fur trade waned, the British Government dispatched the Palliser Expedition to western North America to survey the potential for settlement and commerce. In 1859, James Hector, doctor and geologist to the expedition, climbed an unnamed peak north of Glacier Lake in what is now Banff National Park. Hector's was the last recorded summit ascent until the Canadian Pacific Railway completed its line through the Rockies in 1884. After riding a construction train west into the mountains, Arthur P. Coleman, a professor from Toronto, climbed two peaks on the eastern flank of the Bow Valley – Castle Mountain and Whitehorn Mountain.

In 1885, the Canadian government established Banff National Park on lands adjacent to the newly completed railway. Realizing that the route of the rails made a convenient baseline from which to survey the park and its surroundings, the following year the Department of the Interior assigned three Dominion Land Surveyors to the task: James Joseph (J.J.) McArthur, William Stuart Drewry, and Arthur St. Cyr.

Up until the mid-1800s, landscape surveying was realized through equal measures of science, engineering, and toil. In 1849, the French

Right: J.J. McArthur, 1894

This panoramic view from the summit of Waputik Mountain, probably taken by J.J. McArthur in 1888, is one of the earlier photographs of the upper Bow Valley. The north peak of Mt. Victoria is the high summit on the skyline, right of centre. Mt. Temple is left of centre in the distance, on the edge of the Bow Valley.

surveyor, Ami Laussedat, developed a surveying method that relied on the camera. Although the additional equipment increased the labour of creating maps, there were two distinct payoffs: a quantum leap in accuracy, and a final product with a quality and aesthetic akin to that of a work of art.

Phototopography was refined in Italy, but it would be perfected in the wilds of western Canada. In addition to making the regular measurements of triangulation, surveyors took photographs of the surrounding mountains and valleys whenever they occupied high high points in the landscape. These reference points were called camera stations. To facilitate later identification, they pencilled the date, and sequence of a photograph directly onto the exposed plate before it was processed. By later comparing the photographic views from different camera stations, and by incorporating this information with the standard surveying measurements, the surveyors were able to add a third dimension to their work, producing the first shaded-relief maps in North America. As a consequence they elevated themselves in standing, from surveyors to topographers.

All of the country to be mapped had to be photographed from at least two camera stations. It wasn't always necessary to climb to a summit; sometimes a high point on a ridge would provide unobstructed views. But early on in the work, J.J. McArthur in particular developed a fondness for lugging the cumbersome surveying and photographic gear all the way to the top. As a result he became one of Canada's first practiced mountaineers. McArthur's achievements were remarkable. Working in the brief summers just after the end of the Little Ice Age, and often without benefit

In a 1920 article, surveyor A.O. Wheeler described the financial rationale for phototopography: "The office work occupies at least twice the time of the work in the field. To offset this the field work, which is most expensive, can be done in half the time, or less... In three months of fair weather, from 500 to 1000 square miles of country can be mapped by one party...." This view of Fortress Lake illustrates part of the technique by which photographs were incorporated into surveying. Called "the method of squares," the overlaid grid helped to align images taken from different camera stations.

of trails, he climbed peak after peak. In the five seasons that McArthur worked in the Rockies, between 1887 and 1893, he made some 160 ascents and travelled approximately 2400 kilometres. In 1889 alone, he travelled 650 kilometres, climbed 43 mountains and took 300 glass plate photographs.

W.S. Drewry was no less energetic. In 1890, he trooped all over the mostly blank map – topping Bonnet Peak South in the front ranges of Banff, Mt. Deville and Mt. McArthur in Yoho, and plodding most of the way to the summit of Mt. Hector. He abandoned this last peak, because the final ice slope proved too difficult to ascend with heavy gear. If Drewry had carried on that day, he would have made the first ascent of any Canadian peak over 11,000 feet.

Late in the season, when a surveyor better understood the country, he often reoccupied an outstanding camera station. The surveyors attempted to budget their field time, leaving higher peaks for the odd spells of good weather, while ascending lower peaks on poor weather days. In 1887, J.J. McArthur and his assistant, Tom Riley, made the first ascent of any mountain in Canada over 10,000 feet – Mt. Stephen, near Field. Firesmoke marred the views on that September day. It was five summers before the pair could climb the peak again. This time, they carried a section of tree to leave in the summit cairn as a sighting pole.

In his annual reports, McArthur summarized his prodigious exploits with a kind of descriptive shorthand – perhaps a product of note-taking practiced in harsh field conditions. He recounted his travels of 1888 with just 241 words – he had occupied 23 camera stations. Because many of the mountains that McArthur and his colleagues

climbed were unnamed at the time, and because they often failed to mention the particulars of certain summits in their reports, some of the ascents went uncredited when the first mountaineering guidebook to the Rockies appeared in 1921. In many cases, this lack of official recognition persists, but the surveyors' photographs fill the gaps in their written accounts.

J.J. McArthur excelled in his profession. In the 1890s he served on the commission that surveyed the Canada-Alaska boundary. He later held the office of president of the Association of Dominion Land Surveyors. McArthur died in 1925. Four features in Yoho

Above: Surveyors J.J. McArthur and Tom Riley made the first ascent of Mt. Stephen on September 9, 1887. When the pair returned in 1892 (when this photo was taken), McArthur noted that the upper part of the peak had become easier to climb due to a massive rockslide from the summit ridge.

National Park commemorate him: a lake, a mountain, a pass, and a creek. The splendid McArthur Peak (4344 metres) of the Mt. Logan massif also honours him. Arthur St. Cyr is remembered in the name of a mountain in the northern Selkirk Range. A later surveyor named a mountain in BC's Purcell Range for William Drewry, but the name has not been granted official status.

This map sheet of Castle Mountain, at 1:40,000 scale, published ca. 1892, was in the first series of Canadian maps produced using phototopography. W.S. Drewry carried out the fieldwork; J.J. McArthur plotted the results.

School's Out

They had two things in common: they were enrolled at Yale University, and they fancied themselves explorers. Samuel Allen, five years the younger, had climbed briefly in the Rockies and the Selkirks in 1891 and had topped the Matterhorn in 1892. His companion, Walter Wilcox, had traversed the Rockies by train in 1891 but had never put boot to mountain. The pair met at Banff in 1893. At Allen's prompting, they set off for Lake Louise, where Allen intended to explore the landscape that he had glimpsed two years earlier.

The beginning of their summer vacation was nothing to write home about.

The Lake Louise Chalet – built and operated by the Canadian Pacific Railway – had burned down just prior to their arrival. Allen and Wilcox were obliged to camp on the shore of what Wilcox later described as "a muskeg filled with mosquitoes and tree stumps." There were probably few occasions that summer when the two got the chill and the dampness out of their bones. They reached only one summit – Fairview Mountain – but with the keenness of youth, they covered ground – making the first forays toward Mt. Victoria (then known as Mt. Green), and the first attempt on Mt. Temple. On both peaks they reached altitudes of almost 10,000 feet.

Opposite: Walter Wilcox's reputation as a photographer was in no small part due to the quality of his equipment and his commitment to using it. No "Kodakerist," he packed a cumbersome, 11x14 camera on many of his mountain travels. This view from the early 1900s, entitled "On the North Slope of Pinnacle Mountain," shows the Grand Sentinel and some of its lesser counterparts.

Above: This Vaux family photo of the Lower Victoria Glacier shows conditions much as they would have been for the climbers from Yale in the summers of 1893 and 1894. Mt. Lefroy is central in the view, with The Mitre to the left, and Mt. Victoria to the right. The couloir where Frissell fell is the snow-choked cleft on the lower buttress of Mt. Lefroy, near the right-hand edge of the photograph.

Walter Wilcox's 1909 map of the Lake Louise area showed remarkable detail.

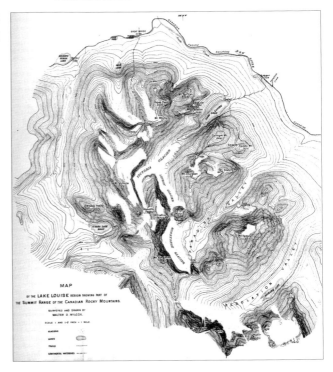

Inspired by the summer of 1893, Allen and Wilcox returned the following year with reinforcements from Yale – Yandell Henderson, George Warrington, and Louis Frissell – all neophyte mountaineers. Wilcox, Allen, and Henderson each left written accounts of their adventures. Henderson compiled his forty years later from letters written home in 1894. He described Warrington as a man who "read more and took less physical exercise than any other." Frissell "wished for adventures and was by nature wholly free from fear of their hazards." Henderson's principal interest was to "bring back the skin of one of the – then almost mythical – white goats of the Rockies." Of the party, Henderson commented: "We had also that spirit of adventure that gets boys into tight places and (generally) gets them out again."

When Henderson, Wilcox, and Frissell arrived, they were the first to occupy the newly constructed – although yet to be furnished – Chalet. They slept on the floor and paid $12.00 per week between them, which included meals, and the use of a pony and a rowboat.

The trio began getting into tight places on the third day when Wilcox led Henderson and Frissell up a couloir on Mt. Lefroy. As they climbed on ledges alongside the rift, Wilcox cautioned Henderson not to touch a particularly large boulder. The second man on the rope neglected to pass the warning along to Frissell who, moments later, slid over the ledge in the company of said boulder. The climbing rope stopped Frissell but "the boulder had no rope [attached] to it and it landed 600 feet below, leaving two holes in the snow-slope 200 feet apart, each as big as an ordinary grave...."

They found Frissell unconscious,

From the very beginning, explorers imbued the Rockies with myth. Reverend William Spotswood Green was the first mountaineer to visit Lake Louise. This dramatic illustration of Lake Louise appeared in his book, *Glaciers of the Selkirks*, published in 1888.

dangling over the ledge. He revived after half an hour but was unable to walk, obligating his companions to lower him down the cliffs and snowslopes to the edge of the glacier. It took two hours, after which Wilcox set off for help, crossing the glacier alone.

Wilcox found only the cook at the Chalet, and so carried on to Laggan (Lake Louise) railway station to telegraph to Banff for help. The cook eventually mustered the Chalet manager and two workers, who, together with Henderson, carried Frissell to the inlet of Lake Louise. There, two railway men sent by Wilcox joined the rescue party. Wilcox and Dr. Brett, Banff's presiding medical man, arrived at the Chalet at midnight. The doctor dismissed Frissell's injury as a torn muscle, and soon saddled up to ride down to Laggan and a train east. The mishap had comic overtones, but it was a grim portent for later climbers.

Frissell was still hobbling about when Allen arrived on July 24. By the end of the month, Warrington had also arrived to make his first outing in the mountains, joining Wilcox, Henderson, and Allen for a stroll on Lower Victoria Glacier. They had been on the ice but a short time when Warrington took his first fall of the day, up to his armpits in a crevasse. Wilcox and Henderson yanked him out. The party turned south onto Lefroy Glacier and ascended to the ridge just east of The Mitre. From the crest they looked south into a meadowed valley "crossed by sparkling brooks." According to Henderson and Wilcox, the idyllic view inspired the name, Paradise Valley. But Allen named it Wastach – Stoney for "beautiful."

Mountaineering in the 1890s, as now, had a few general principles that helped ensure longevity. But the young men from Yale apparently had too little

It may appear idyllic, but Yandell Henderson called it "Starvation Camp." Variously occupied by all five members of the Yale Lake Louise Club in the second and third weeks of August 1894, this tent served as the base for the first ascents of Mt. Aberdeen and Mt. Temple, and for the first crossings of Sentinel, Wastach, and Wenkchemna passes. The campsite occupied a wet meadow that sloped toward Paradise Creek. The Yale group set a soggy precedent that lasted nearly a century — the national park backcountry campsite in Paradise Valley soaked up the same spot until 1983.

mountaineering experience to hold any of these tenets deeply. Instead of returning over familiar ground from the high point of their outing, they plunged south with youthful zeal onto the massive snowslope that led down into the new valley.

Warrington – third on the rope – soon tripped. The pull on the rope toppled Allen, who landed on his fallen mate. The pair slid into Wilcox, knocking him over. Then

Henderson joined all the falling bodies. The impromptu group toboggan session was only arrested when Henderson and Wilcox dug their heels into the slope. Henderson considered the close call to be "the funniest thing I was ever in."

The group split up in the new valley: Wilcox and Henderson returned to the Chalet over Saddleback Pass, Allen stayed with Warrington, who had become lame. When night fell they were "in a wretched place upon a steep bank strewn with fallen timber." They "await-

"Frissell got [in] a little tumble on Thursday (July 12) and we thought for a while he might have cracked his hip. But it proved to be only a muscle injury and in a week or two he will be all right. I made him a crutch this morning and he hobbles around cheerfully." The members of the Yale Lake Louise Club are, l-r, Henderson, Frissell, Warrington, and Wilcox.

Samuel Allen took this self-portrait on August 11, 1894, in the upper Prospector's Valley, looking north toward Opabin Pass. He was truly alone; his companions were some 25 km away at the Chalet Lake Louise.

ed the dawn in silent misery," coaxing a pathetic fire.

A few days later, Henderson and Allen returned to Paradise Valley. It took them two days to reach the upper valley, where they pitched the group's tent in a swampy meadow. The next day, the pair made a circuit over Sentinel and Wastach passes – taking the first steps in the upper Valley of the Ten Peaks. This time it was Henderson who took a fall, on the ice slope north of Wastach Pass. He made light of the mishap, noting that, "In such tumbles a twelve-pound rifle on one's back is something of a handicap." But Allen recorded that his companion came to rest with his "feet dangling over a bergschrund [crevasse]...." Henderson would not climb again.

The pair completed the outing in a downpour, and were eating dinner when Wilcox arrived ahead of Frissell. Henderson set off to find Frissell, missed him in the dark, and returned to camp to find the new arrivals trying to kindle a fire with wet wood. Sharp words must have been exchanged, for in his account, Henderson remarked: "Allen and I should have cut fire wood that morning, instead of going off exploring."

Warrington – no doubt deterred by his first hike in the mountains – was still at the Chalet. Henderson volunteered next day to take horses and pick him up. He completed the last five kilometres with the benefit of a new trail; the campfire that Allen and Warrington had supposedly doused after their night out, had grown into an inferno and razed 400 acres of forest. Twenty railway men had beaten a trail to the blaze to fight it. (A few weeks later, Henderson – apparently not quite equating cause and effect – blithely reported that Rocky Mountains Park had stationed a member of the North West Mounted Police at the Chalet, with the reported instruction to prevent forest fires.)

By the time he reached the Chalet, Henderson was tree weary and

Fifty years before crampons, the solution to poor traction was to nail the soles of climbing boots. Many accounts exist of climbers leaving trails of sparks as they scrambled up desperate parts of cliffs. Their only hope, should they fall, was a manila rope tied about the waist.

drenched. He and Warrington passed a leisurely day before returning to their companions, noting that "as the other fellows have eleven loaves of bread and two cans of corned beef, they could live another day without us."

When they returned to Paradise Valley it would be the only time that all five schoolmates were together in the backcountry, and it lasted but a few days. Wilcox "boiled the tea and destroyed the sleep of the party for a night." Henderson used corn meal to make hoe cakes, which everyone gobbled up. Allen promptly attempted to duplicate the recipe, but missed the key step of pre-soaking the meal in boiling water. Henderson could remember the stomach ache 40 years later. Their two Stoney horse packers spat out the cuisine and fled.

The group began another ragged retreat, naming the site "Starvation Camp" for the fare, which had consisted of "raw corn meal and porcupine soup." Each man took his own route and time. Allen arrived at the Chalet a day after the others, having made what the late Jon Whyte rightly called "the single greatest day of Canadian Rockies exploration." Allen had crossed Wastach and Wenkchemna passes to upper Prospector's Valley, then ascended the south lobe of Opabin Glacier to the crest of Opabin Pass. From there he became the first white explorer to view the Lake O'Hara area. The outing was an indicator of Allen's resolve, and served as a warm-up for further exploration. In early September, after the others left the Rockies, Allen journeyed to Lake O'Hara from the north with a companion named Yule Carryer. On that outing, the pair became the first to climb to the crest of Abbot Pass, and to Wiwaxy Gap.

Warrington could not be enticed to join the others when they again returned to Paradise Valley in the third

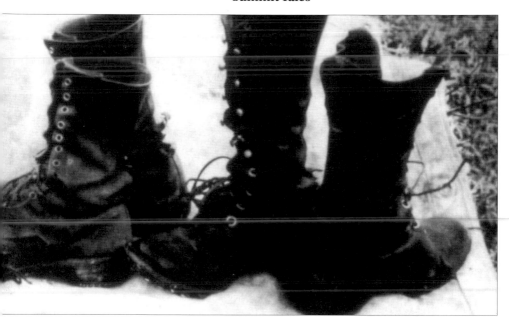

week of August. He remained at the Chalet reading Shakespeare while Wilcox, Allen, and Frissell climbed Mt. Aberdeen and Mt. Temple – the latter being the first ascent of any Canadian mountain over 11,000 feet.

Not many landmarks near Lake Louise bore names at the beginning of the summer of 1894. Mt. Victoria was known as Mt. Green; Fairview Mountain as Goat Mountain. Those few explorers who knew the landscape well enough quibbled over which was Mt. Lefroy and which was Mt. Temple. Wilcox and Allen willingly filled the toponymical void. Most of the place-names they bestowed were descriptive, but Allen departed from standard practice by choosing names that he claimed were "Waes-

gabee," or Stoney (a Lakota/Nakoda dialect). Allen had learned these names from various Stoneys that he and Wilcox employed in 1893 and 1894.

In some cases, Wilcox and Allen each assigned a different name to the same feature. The competition ruined an already spirited relationship. Realizing that the first published

"...He was moody and loved solitude, studying the mountains in their details all day long with a pair of glasses... His best work was the crossing of Opabin Pass and his explorations around Lake O'Hara. As for the Ten Peaks, he has left a legacy that has confused every mountaineer for the last thirty years." Walter Wilcox's appraisal of Samuel Allen in 1925 was typical of their relationship – part praise and part the bearing of a grudge. Allen was a brilliant man. He passed the Yale entrance exam at age 16, and by age 20 held an M.A.

This view, taken August 18, 1893, shows typical climbing attire and equipment of the 1890s. Samuel Allen is second from the left, with C.S. Thompson (centre) and H.P. Nichols (second from right). The two men flanking the trio are porters employed at Glacier House, where this photograph – the only one in this book not of the Rockies – was taken. With this scant equipment, the climbers were about to depart for the first ascent of Mt. Fox in the Selkirks – an outing that required three days.

account of the Lake Louise region might formalize the place-names, Allen and Wilcox each hurried to get a version into print. In terms of timing, the contest was a tie, but Allen chose to publish his account in an elite publication not available to many – the British *Alpine Journal* – whereas Wilcox's lavishly illustrated, book-length work was widely distributed. *Camping in the Rockies*, later titled *The Rockies of Canada*, went through three editions and numerous printings, establishing Wilcox as the authority on the area. By the third edition, only four references remained to Samuel Allen in all of its 330 pages. The map it included was surprisingly accurate, especially when compared to Allen's privately published drawing, which, among other things, confused matters by placing north at the bottom, and by incorrectly locating Mt. Lefroy and Mt. Temple.

Wilcox continued to visit the Rock-

ies until the 1940s. He wrote the first guidebook to the Lake Louise area, and played an important role in early exploration north from the railway. He died in 1949. Three features – a pass, a mountain, and a creek – commemorate him. Allen, only 21 years old in 1895, showed potential to be among the great explorers of the Rockies when he made an epic trek to Mt. Assiniboine. From his published account, it was clear that he intended to return to the mountains, but his parents disapproved. The young Yale graduate suffered from what has variously been reported as a mental breakdown, senile dementia, or schizophrenia. Correspondence written by Allen exists from 1897, but soon thereafter he was confined to an institution, where he languished until his death in 1945. As a final irony, *Shappee*, Peak Six of Allen's Wenkchemna Peaks (named for the numbers 1 to 10 in the Stoney language) now bears his name.

Little changed in the way of attire and equipment in the 13 years following the first ascent of Mt. Temple. Although this climber is at the base of the "regular route" up Mt. Temple, he is not intent on the summit. He is taking part in "the tour of the passes" — a popular two-day loop outing from Lake Louise that crossed Mitre, Sentinel, Wenkchemna, Opabin, and Abbot passes.

Fall and Redemption

In 1894 there were relatively few people in North America who considered themselves mountaineers. This cadre was beginning to focus on the Canadian Rockies, so it was not surprising that a chance encounter between three key figures took place that summer at Lake Louise. Walter Wilcox and Samuel Allen had just returned to the Chalet from their successful ascent of Mt. Temple. At dinner, they met Charles Ernest Fay and a companion. Fay was a professor of Modern Languages at Tufts University, and president of the Appalachian Mountain Club (AMC) – at the time, the only mountaineering organization in North America.

Fay and his friend were making a whistle stop at the Chalet on their way home from climbing in the Selkirk Mountains and on Mt. Stephen near Field. Allen joined Fay for a rowboat excursion on Lake Louise, and attempted to persuade the professor to climb what was then known as Mt. Green – today's Mt. Victoria. The 48 year-old Fay considered the mountain out of his league and declined given the constraints of his schedule. But Allen's excitement for the peaks near Lake Louise, in concert with the view from the rowboat, must have planted a seed, for Fay would be back the following year and for 23 summers to follow.

Opposite: The Kaufmann brothers of Grindelwald worked in the Rockies between 1900 and 1906, and were involved in the first ascents of many of the highest peaks. This photograph, probably taken in 1904, shows Christian — who always cut a more dashing figure than Hans — on the lower Victoria Glacier, with the notorious couloir of Mt. Lefroy to the left.

Above: Mt. Lefroy is central in this view taken in 1902, with Abbot Pass to the right. The west face of Mt. Lefroy, where Abbot fell, is concealed behind the right-hand skyline of the mountain.

This previously unpublished photograph portrays key figures in the mountaineering history of the Rockies. Peter Sarbach is in the foreground, left. J. Norman Collie, Charles Fay, Charles Thompson, and Harold Dixon (l-r) are the others. Collie holds in his hands a camera, Fay a tea cup. Collie and Fay are unroped, suggesting that the photo was taken on the summit of Mt. Gordon in 1897, just before Thompson fell into a crevasse. The only other possible location is the summit of Mt. Lefroy.

The AMC contingent was 20-strong when it commandeered the Chalet in 1895. With one exception, Fay's cohort was utterly green. The practiced mountaineer was Philip Stanley Abbot, a Harvard Law School graduate who had climbed in the Alps, and whom Fay later described as "undoubtedly the most experienced alpinist among American lovers of the sport." Fay, Abbot, and Charles Thompson completed the first ascent of Mt. Hector on July 30. This was Thompson's first alpine climb and the second highest summit reached in Canada. The trio moved to Field to make the third ascent of Mt. Stephen, avenging Fay's failure on the peak the previous year. Their last serious climbs were on Mt. Lefroy, where, without knowing it, they ascended the same couloir in which Frissell had fallen in 1894. A late start curtailed the attempt. That evening, they were apprised of the route's notorious history, and resolved to attempt the summit again the next day. But this foray also proved unsuccessful.

Mt. Victoria is the centrepiece in the view across Lake Louise, but among early mountaineers, only Samuel Allen held a fascination for climbing it. Everyone else was intent on getting to the top of Mt. Victoria's southerly neighbour, Mt. Lefroy. This mountain owed its celebrated status to a mistaken identity. In 1858, James Hector applied

This previously unpublished image shows the summit view from Deltaform Mountain on the occasion of its first ascent in 1903. Hungabee Mountain is prominent.

the name, Mt. Lefroy, to a lofty peak he saw when looking northwest from the Bow Valley near Castle Junction. The peak presently known as Mt. Lefroy is not visible from there. Hector probably intended the name for the mountain we now know as Mt. Temple – a name given by surveyor George Dawson in 1884. When Dawson later drew his map of the Lake Louise area, he applied the name Lefroy to the mountain adjacent to Mt. Victoria.

In 1888, surveyor J.J. McArthur reported that the elevation of Mt. Lefroy was 3553 metres, and stated that it was the highest of the Rocky Mountains in British North America. We can be relatively certain that McArthur was describing Mt. Temple; his measurement was much closer (within 10 metres) to the presently accepted elevation of that mountain, than it was to the elevation of today's Mt. Lefroy. Although it seems unlikely, this implies that McArthur – considered the most knowledgeable person of his day on the Rockies – had not seen Dawson's map, which clearly showed Mt. Temple as the dominant peak of the Lake Louise area. So McArthur unintentionally advertised the wrong peak to the mountaineering community.

That community was eager for the prize. With Abbot now championing the cause, the trio from the AMC returned in August 1896, adding George

Right: Herschel C. Parker of the American Alpine Club snapped this picture of the Kaufmann brothers at the summit of Hungabee Mountain during the first ascent in 1903. Christian is on the left.

Opposite: The novelty of alpine climbing and the desire for a good "Kodak" of the moment often combined to put early climbers in harm's way. This group from the Alpine Club of Canada, Sherbrooke Valley camp of 1911, is strolling along a cornice on Mt. Daly, with a 400 metre drop beneath the apex of the snow.

Little to their team. Abbot wanted to forge a new route on Mt. Lefroy by ascending the Lower Victoria Glacier to its culmination on the saddle between Mt. Lefroy and Mt. Victoria. Samuel Allen had named the saddle, "Death Trap Col," on account of the avalanches that poured into its approaches on the Lake Louise side.

The foursome departed the Chalet by rowboat at 6:15 AM on August 3. By 11:50 AM they stood on the crest of the col. After surveying the west face of Mt. Lefroy, Abbot exclaimed, "The peak is ours!" The climbers were so confident, they took a leisurely lunch, and then cached their remaining food and blankets on the pass.

The icy west face of Mt. Lefroy rises only 420 metres, but the afternoon disappeared in a protracted session of step-cutting. Each climber moved one step at a time up the zigzag staircase that Abbot cleaved from the mountain-

side. Near the summit, a series of parallel rock buttresses protruded from the slope, separated by icy gullies. Abbot elected to take to the rock, hoping to save time. Before he set off up a narrow crack, he directed Thompson and Fay, third and fourth on the rope, to untie and to take shelter from falling rocks. As Little prepared to follow, the rope between him and Abbot dislodged a rock that hit the lower man. Then a larger rock fell on the rope, nearly severing it. So Abbot asked Little to unrope and to clamber up to join him.

Little met Abbot on a rocky shelf that led off to the climbers' left. Abbot moved in that direction to another vertical crack. When Little asked if the shelf might not provide an end-run around the cliff, Abbot replied: "I think not. I have a good lead here." A few moments later, Little saw something fall past him. Downslope, Fay and Thompson watched in horror as Abbot, plummet-

ing backward and head down, pitched into the slope within a few metres of them, cartwheeled over, and began rolling down the incline, the climbing rope curling about him. Fay later speculated that the rope provided enough friction to arrest Abbot's tumble, the trajectory of which would otherwise have launched him off a cliff.

It was Little who broke the pall: "Never mind me. Hurry to help Abbot!" Fay and Thompson would not honour his request. Little was 30 feet above them and did not have the benefit of a rope to belay himself down the cliff. Little did most of the down-climbing on his own, but Fay and Thompson assisted the final moves by placing their ice axes under his feet and thighs to serve as holds. It was 6:30 PM before the three shocked climbers were reunited and could begin their unroped descent of the icy slope, the grim spectre of their fallen comrade before them. They reached Abbot in three hours and were amazed to find him alive. But after they gently extricated him from

The two guides — Rudolf Aemmer (l) and Ed Feuz Jr. (on top) — and the two climbers — Basil Darling and Val Fynn — were a "who's who" of mountaineering in 1911. Two years later, Darling was in a party that very nearly made the second ascent of Mt. Robson. The group is atop a pinnacle on the south ridge of Mt. Victoria.

Right: Two mountains near Lake Louise — Pinnacle Mountain and The Mitre — were considered climbing test pieces in the early 1900s. Two of Edward Whymper's guides first climbed The Mitre in 1901. In this view, taken in 1910 when the mountain still possessed some of its shine, guide Rudolph Aemmer (l) stands at the summit with his client, Rollin T. Chamberlin.

Opposite: J. Norman Collie leads a rope through one of the icefalls on Bow Glacier during the first ascent of Mt. Gordon in 1897.

the rope and prepared to carry him down, their companion succombed to his injuries. Abbot had been less than a month from his 29th birthday.

In the dark, with weather rapidly deteriorating, Fay, Thompson, and Little climbed back to the crest of the col, where they took meager shelter behind the cairn built two years earlier by Yule Carryer. At first light, Fay found their packs under a dusting of snow. After a quick meal, the party descended to the Chalet. Thompson carried on to Laggan, where he telegraphed Abbot's father.

Although Philip Abbot was the first North American to die on this continent from a fall while climbing, he was not the first to perish on a mountain. Records show that between 1849 and 1890, at least seven people died from hypothermia, drowning, or being struck by falling ice on Mt. Washington in New Hampshire. Nevertheless, within a day of Abbot's demise the arcane

pursuit of mountaineering came under intense scrutiny. Cries for its abolition echoed from soapboxes and from editorial pages. A few months into the debate, Fay summoned the resolve to state the case of mountaineers: "... after duly weighing all that is urged against Alpine climbing and while appreciating, none more profoundly, the value of the rare life that went out on Mt. Lefroy, we maintain that the gain therefrom for the general and for the individual life in an age of growing carefulness for ease and luxury must be held to outweigh the deplorable losses, and that this casualty should not call a halt in American alpinism." Surprisingly, Abbot's father, a well-connected railway magnate, supported this view. He soon began advocating another attempt on Mt. Lefroy, to prove that misfortune had played the key role in his son's death, and that the peak was achievable by talented mountaineers.

The Canadian Pacific Railway (CPR)

pursued its own self-interest in the controversy. The CPR operated five mountain hotels, including the Chalet at Lake Louise. For four summers, the company had been catering to the whims of mountaineers – arranging packers and supplies, cutting trails, putting out forest fires, providing rides on hand-cars, stopping trains between stations to let climbers on and off. In return, the climbers wrote accounts of their adventures, enticing more visitors to explore the Rockies from the hotels. The CPR wanted to ensure that its clients returned safely from their mountain adventures. The profession of mountain guiding was well established in Europe. It was clearly time to import some of that expertise.

But it was not the CPR that brought the first European mountain guide to the Rockies, it was an Englishman – Harold B. Dixon – who had climbed with Philip Abbot in the Alps. In 1896, Abbot had asked Dixon to join the AMC attempt on Mt. Lefroy, but Dixon was already booked. Aware of the connection between Abbot and Dixon, Fay invited the Englishman to join the attempt on Mt. Lefroy planned for August 1897. Eager to see what kind of mountain had claimed his friend, Dixon agreed, and extended the invitation to the distinguished English alpinist, John Norman Collie. Because he was uncertain of the climbing ability of the Americans who would be on the trip, Dixon also invited Peter Sarbach, a Swiss guide with whom he and Abbot had climbed in the Alps. Fay and five others from the AMC rounded out the contingent. Although the deck was stacked in favour of alpenstock, hemp rope, and hob-nailed boots, Dixon fretted over equipment: "The American continent has not yet superseded the effete countries of Europe in articles connected with the climber's craft. Collie and I spent some serious hours over lists of impedimenta and eatables."

Byron Harmon became the official photographer of the Alpine Club of Canada at its inception in 1906. By 1909, when this photograph was taken on Daly Glacier, the peaks of the Continental Divide

The organization paid off. What was so remarkable about the first ascent of Mt. Lefroy, achieved on August 3, 1897, was not that the party of nine reached the top, but that they did so when intended – exactly one year to the day after Abbot's fall. Considering the vagaries of weather, and the complications of trans-oceanic and transcontinental travel, the logistics of the feat surpassed the difficulty of the climb. With Samuel Allen's later consent, the party renamed "Death Trap Col" as Abbot Pass – the only feature in the Rockies that commemorates Philip Abbot.

Two days later, four climbers, including Collie, Fay, and Sarbach, made the first ascent of Mt. Victoria, with Collie leading the rope. In his accounts, Collie barely mentioned the climbing. Instead, he focused on the distant view north, which included the icy crown of another peak named by James Hector – Mt. Balfour.

Collie had agreed to join the 1897 expedition if he could command the services of Peter Sarbach after the ascent of Mt. Lefroy. With that obliga-tion met, and with the arrival of Collie's friend George Baker, the Anglo-American contingent set off north up the Bow Valley, hoping to find and ascend Mt. Balfour. Instead, in the blank on the map north of Lake Louise, the mountain that Collie's party climbed was the peak now known as Mt. Gordon.

The success was tainted, for even the presence of Peter Sarbach did not prevent another calamity. The entire party was wandering around unroped near the summit when Charles Thompson – last of a group of five to cross a snowbridge – fell into a crevasse. He wedged upside down, almost 20 metres below the surface, with only his left arm free. As those already across the crevasse did not have a climbing rope, they could not come to his aid. They began calling for the help of their companions still on the summit, eventually securing their attention when Sarbach noticed that the distant group consisted of only four climbers instead of five.

In the brief conference that followed, Collie – who was unmarried and who proclaimed his weight as "nine

had become a playground for club members. One or two guides would be in charge of a group like this, many of whose members had never set foot on a glacier.

stone six" (60 kilograms) – volunteered to plumb the icy depths. He put one foot in a stirrup loop and secured another bight of rope around his waist. Lowered into the crevasse, Collie eventually came feet to feet with Thompson, but could do little for him. The crevasse was so narrow, Collie had to raise his own arms over his head to keep them free. He called for another rope. When the end of the rope arrived, Collie, with great difficulty, tied a noose in it. "With this I lassoed that poor pathetic arm which was the only part of Thompson that could be seen. Then came the tug-of war." Brute force prevailed. The pull from above freed Thompson, then righted him, then propelled him back to the land of the living. Collie soon followed. The pair became lifelong friends.

This rescue was pivotal in the history of mountaineering in the Rockies – more so than Abbot's death. Had the group not been able to haul Thompson from the crevasse, he would soon have perished, and the argument that mountain guides made climbing in the Rockies any safer would have been gutted and sealed in that icy tomb with him.

Close call or no, Sarbach's involvement in the successes of 1897 bolstered the CPR's intent to bring European guides to Canada. The company required another year to sort out the contractual details. In 1899, Edward Feuz (FOITS) Sr., Christian Häsler Sr., and a Swiss with

"In Philip Abbot high intellectual attainments were combined with a singular nobility of character. Simple, courageous, a keen lover of nature, no wonder such a man delighted in the mountains." Harold B. Dixon

Right: Peter Sarbach of St. Niklaus, the first Swiss guide to work in Canada, 1897

Opposite: Early mountaineers considered Pinnacle Mountain near Lake Louise to be a "trophy" that attested to their rock climbing skills. To ensure bragging rights, the guides fixed a rope in a difficult chimney near the summit. Swiss guide, Christian Häsler Jr., climbs on the upper part of the peak in 1919.

an English name – Charlie Clarke – arrived at Glacier House in Rogers Pass. Feuz and Häsler established the profession of Canadian mountain guiding when they led the first ascent of Mt. Dawson on August 13, with Charles Fay as one of their clients. The following year, the CPR brought guides to Mt. Stephen House at Field, and finally, two years later, to the Chalet at Lake Louise, where the railway company's guiding operation would enjoy its greatest longevity.

The CPR's mountain guides, most of whom were Swiss, initially stayed in Canada only during the summers. In 1911, the CPR hit upon the idea of employing the guides to take care of its vacant hotels in winter. One of the principal jobs was stocking the ice houses. The CPR continued to employ European mountain guides until 1954. In the 55 years that the guides worked in Canada, despite the inevitable mishaps and tumbles, not a single client died during thousands of ascents. Most prominent among the guides was Edward Feuz Jr., who worked from 1903 to 1944, and who led 78 first ascents in the Rockies and Selkirks. But Christian Kaufmann of Grindelwald was the guide who, through the fortune of timing, skimmed the cream. Part of his tally of more than 30 first ascents between 1900 and 1906 still reads like a mountaineer's wish list: Assiniboine, Columbia, Lyell, Freshfield, Forbes, Bryce, Hungabee, Huber, and Deltaform.

Although it was often the lot of the guides to ply trade routes on the mountains around Lake Louise, they also participated in many first ascents of peaks distant from the hotels and the railway. Collectively, their care, skill, and industry redeemed Abbot's fall of 1896, abetted the exploration of the Rockies, and established mountaineering as a legitimate recreational pursuit.

A Careful Study

It was a fortunate coincidence of history, science, and climate; the early tourists in the Rockies arrived with the first portable, dry-process cameras in their luggage, at the time when many glaciers had just begun to shrink from their recent maximums. Although photography was still a decade away from "Kodakery," the advancements in the technology had transformed it from a discipline that required the patience of Job and the skills of a chemist, to one where concerns for lighting and composition could be paramount to the process of exposing the plates, using equipment that could be lugged to the tops of mountains.

Many of what are today moraine fields in the Rockies were, in the late 1880s, still flush with glacial ice. Although we marvel at the lengthwise ablation of glaciers since that time – in some cases, they have melted back as much as five kilometers – it is more difficult to grasp their reduction in breadth and in height. The overall decrease in ice mass since the 1880s is staggering – as much as 25 percent at the Columbia Icefield and in the upper Bow Valley. Glaciologists can gauge this variation by measuring the heights of moraine crests left behind by the retreating ice, and by studying ice-contact trees in nearby forests. In the photographs taken by tourists and explorers of the day, a more immediate portrait of the glaciers and their subsequent recession is revealed.

Among the most important documentary photographs from that time are those of the Vaux (VOX) family. George Vaux Sr. and his three children, Mary, George Jr., and William, first saw the Rockies and the Selkirk Mountains

---

Opposite: This view of Bow Glacier in 1902 is a an intriguing photograph, shot into the glare of sun glinting off ice – the three, ice-walking figures and the dog barely discernible. The image transcends the constraints of film – Bow Glacier has receded two kilometres since it was taken. If not for this photograph and a few others of its era, our knowledge of the recent glacial past at

Bow Lake would be nothing but a jumble of moraines and the dry discourses of glaciologists.

Above: It was a Vaux family photographic trademark to put people into the alien world of glacial ice. Mary Vaux poses at the emergence of a subglacial stream at Yoho Glacier – the very source of the Yoho River

William Vaux is either camera-shy or is composing an image; George Jr. is third from the left. Two friends and two guides round out the party — Christian Häsler is on the right. Mary Vaux took this photograph on Victoria Glacier, July 7, 1900.

in 1887. Initially, little separated the Vauxes from the typical travelling gentry. But after a return visit to the area in 1894, the Quaker family from Philadelphia became members of a self-proclaimed "Rocky Mountain cult." What prompted this conversion was a comparison of photographs of the Illecillewaet Glacier at Rogers Pass taken in 1887 with those of the same subject taken on their second trip. In seven years, the glacier had shrunk dramatically. In that decline the Vauxes recognized an opportunity; their collective creativity became ascendant, inspiring their future visits to the mountains.

In 1837, the Swiss-born naturalist Louis Agassiz had first proposed his theory of ice-ages, asserting that most northern landscapes had once been buried in ice. After a frigid fury that lasted five decades, the doctrine of Agassiz had been largely embraced in Europe. Elsewhere, though, the documentation of glacial cause and effect remained an uncracked gem: glaciology did not yet exist as a separate discipline of science. The Vaux family became its first practitioners in North America. Their passion for glacier study embodied the spirit of the late-Victorian era. They were amateurs with a mission – to contrib-

ute to science, to explore new ground, and to enjoy themselves thoroughly in the process.

William spent much of the winter of 1897-98 studying what had been written about glaciers, so that when they visited Glacier House in the Selkirks the following summer, the Vaux family could begin a detailed photographic documentation using accepted techniques. They were the first in North America to practice what is now called repeat photography. By returning – 11 times in the next 14 years – to precise locations, aligning their cameras along compass bearings, exposing photographs at the same time of day, and using the same lenses to capture comparable lighting conditions and equivalent fields of view, they were able to record the incremental recession of the Illecillewaet, Asulkan, Victoria, and Yoho glaciers. William and George Jr. took most of the photographs. Mary processed the plates and printed from them, and painted the glass images that the Vauxes projected as lantern slides to illustrate their talks on the mountains.

The Canadian Pacific Railway (CPR) assisted the family in their work, supplying equipment and people to help with the surveys, and providing

Mary Vaux stands proudly on the summit of Mt. Stephen on July 21, 1900, with guides, Ed Feuz Sr. and Christian Häsler Sr. Mary and George took a 360° panorama from the summit, a photographic vista unequalled since.

rail passes. In gratitude, the Vauxes donated a publication to the railway – *The Glaciers of the Canadian Rockies & Selkirks* – which the CPR used for promotion. Back at home in Philadelphia, the Vaux family gave electric lantern shows of their images, exhibited at galleries, and incorporated their work into eight published monographs. William's publication, *Modern Glaciers* was cited by the Commission Internationale des Glaciers.

Whereas William was more inclined to study the ice rivers from the valley bottoms, George Jr. and Mary began taking cameras to the heights in 1899. The following year, George Jr. became the first "amateur" mountaineer to ascend Mt. Sir Donald in the Selkirks. On July 21 that year, he and Mary climbed Mt. Stephen, the first time a woman reached a summit over 10,000 feet in Canada. Mary was also the first woman to traverse Abbott Pass, and the first to cross the Wapta Icefield.

After William's death from tuberculosis in 1908, Mary and George Jr. continued the glacier study. In 1914, Mary, then 54, married Charles Walcott, Secretary of the Smithsonian Institution and discoverer of the Burgess Shale. With Walcott's assistance, the Smithsonian published Mary's *North American Wildflowers* in 1925, as a five volume set of 400 prints. Hailed as the "Audubon of botany," at the time, it was the most comprehensive botanical work on the continent. With printing costs of $236,000, it was also one of the more expensive books published to that date. Although Mary continued to visit the Rockies, and to update the CPR's pamphlet, the glacier study waned. Arthur Wheeler, president of the Alpine Club of Canada, took over measurements of the Yoho Glacier until the late 1920s, when glacial recession prevented access to the ice.

In their enthusiasm for all things mountain, the Vaux family helped introduce many to the Rockies, including explorer Mary Schäffer, and mountaineers Charles Fay and Samuel Allen. In the landscape, all that remains of their energy are a few weathered paint marks that bear witness to where the ice once stood. But in the Archives and Library of the Whyte Museum of the Canadian Rockies, some 3000 images of their work endure, along with field notes, correspondence, and maps – a testimony to scientific and creative advance at the onset of glacial decline.

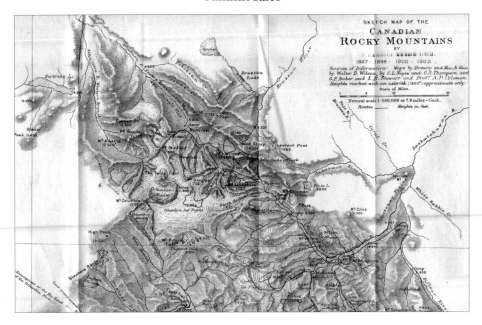

Bushed and Humbugged

I. Three Times Lucky

"A HIGH MOUNTAIN is always seductive, but a mountain with a mystery is doubly so."

With these words, Arthur P. Coleman began his story of the quest for Mt. Hooker and Mt. Brown, once thought to be the highest mountains between Mexico and Alaska. Coleman, a professor from the University of Toronto, had made the first climbs in what is now Banff National Park, when he ascended Castle Mountain and Whitehorn

Mountain in 1884.

Coleman's interest in Mt. Hooker and Mt. Brown stemmed from the account of David Douglas, the botanist (for whom the Douglas-fir is named) who tagged along with an eastbound fur trade brigade in 1827. On May 1, Douglas slogged up a peak on the west side of Athabasca Pass. When he returned to England, he named the peak Mt. Brown, and described it as being 16,000 feet high. A neighbouring peak to the east, which he named Mt. Hooker, he reported to be 15,700

Opposite: A.P. Coleman did not carry a camera on his first five expeditions in the Rockies. The only illustrations of those outings are pencil sketches and watercolours, in which the geologist revealed a talent in the visual arts that rivaled his affinity for the earth sciences. This sketch is a "mind's-eye" view of his party attempting Mt. Brazeau, the highest peak in the front ranges, in 1902.

Above: J. Norman Collie incorporated information from the maps and travels of eight other topographers and mountaineers in his remarkable 1903 depiction of the central Rockies. It remained the best map of the area for two decades.

feet high. But Coleman wondered: Why had nobody else during the fur trade, and no railway surveyors who visited Athabasca Pass in 1872, mentioned two such fantastic peaks? In 1891, Coleman resolved to find the mythic mountains. The account of his first attempt is often overlooked. It is a story that reveals the wildness of the country, the perils of underestimating it, and the mettle of the man.

"In order to get there one had, it appeared, only to canoe seventy miles down the Columbia [River] from Beavermouth [station] on the railway, and then follow the old portage trail up Wood River to the [Athabasca] pass... Frank Stover, whom I persuaded to join me, had excellent reasons for going. He had never paddled a canoe, nor climbed a mountain, nor shot a grizzly, and earnestly desired to do these things." A few days later, the easy paddling on the Columbia River ended at Surprise Rapids. The tangled undergrowth on the riverbanks concealed the portage trail. Coleman's view became more realistic. "It was evident that our expedition was to be no holiday trip... We decided to climb the nearest peak of the Selkirks and get a chance to look down on our enemy."

The view from the summit, which the pair reached two days later, revealed more whitewater downriver. Coleman and Stover descended, and after trying again to portage around the rapids, built a raft and recklessly attempted to run the torrent. The raft soon flipped. The river would easily have killed both men had they not managed to cling to the craft as the current kicked it out into an eddy six kilometres downstream. Their two packs dangled from the ruined raft by a shred of rawhide. After drying out their gear, the pair carried on. Six days later, Coleman sized up the grub pile. "Our appetites had played us

the usual trick of growing with the hard work." It would be a common refrain during early mountaineering trips in the Rockies – the food usually ran out before the explorers even glimpsed their objectives.

Returning to Donald railway station a week later, "only the baggagemaster recognised us, after looking us over from head to foot, and asked with a twinkle if we had climbed Mount Brown... we had not... which was a disappointment, but we had settled that a canoe was not the most desirable conveyance to Athabasca Pass...."

Trading canoe for cayuse, in 1892 Coleman attempted to approach Athabasca Pass from the east. He employed two Stoney guides who proved invaluable in getting the party to the North Saskatchewan River, but soon revealed that they knew nothing of the country beyond. Coleman could see that the guides were leading the group away from the mountains. At the mouth of the Brazeau River, the professor took over the routefinding and steered the party back toward higher ground. Coleman and a companion, Louis Stewart, climbed an assortment of peaks along the Brazeau River. From one summit, they saw the crest of a glaciated dome to the west – the first recorded glimpse of the Columbia Icefield – and a high peak to the north that they thought might be Mt. Hooker.

At length, the party crossed Poboktan Pass and descended into a new valley – the Sunwapta. This they followed northwest to its junction with the Athabasca Valley, which they mistakenly thought was the route to Athabasca Pass. (It is the Whirlpool Valley, not the Athabasca Valley, that leads to Athabasca Pass.) After turning up the Athabasca Valley, they took another fork – the Chaba River – which brought them to Fortress Lake on the Continental

Divide. "We were cross as we lit a fire and made supper, and all sorts of doubts troubled us as to our position." Try as he might, Coleman could not make the landscape fit the description of Athabasca Pass, where a tiny tarn called The Committee Punch Bowl was said to occupy the height of land. Fortress Lake was 11 kilometres long, and although wonderful mountains graced the view, none was of fantastic height. After exploring Fortress Lake, the party turned for home. They had travelled more than 800 kilometres and had made 12 first ascents, but they had raised more questions than they had answered.

Coleman built on his failures with innovation. To make the river crossings safer, in 1893 he packed a folding canvas boat. At first, he and his companions made relatively good time, taking a shorter route to the Sunwapta Valley. But they missed the confluence of the Whirlpool River with the Athabasca River – an oversight that cost them four days and 80 kilometres. When they found the Whirlpool Valley they picked up the old voyageur trail, which they followed to Athabasca Pass.

From a pool on the crest of the pass, Coleman observed that one stream flowed north to the Whirlpool Valley, and another flowed to the south. "We were on the Great Divide, the ridge pole of North America, but we felt no enthusiasm... If this was the [Committee] Punch Bowl, where were the giant mountains Brown and Hooker?... We saw commonplace mountains with nothing distinguished in their appearance, undoubtedly lower than half a dozen peaks we had climbed as incidents along the way... We had reached our point after six weeks of toils and anxiety, after three summers of effort, and we did not even raise a cheer. Mount Brown and Mount Hooker were frauds, and we were disgusted at

having been humbugged by them."

Coleman and his companions had hoped to row their canvas boat in a victory cruise at the summit of Athabasca Pass, but considered The Committee Punch Bowl too trifling for the effort. Suffering from a wrenched knee, Coleman did not even bother to join the others as they made the second ascent of Mt. Brown.

II. WITHERING HEIGHTS

EARLY EXPLORATION in the Rockies followed a curious pattern: individual explorers learned from their own mistakes, but were seldom wiser for the blunders of others. A.P. Coleman's exploits of 1893 – which he documented in an article published in 1895 – should have debunked the myth of Mt. Hooker and Mt. Brown. But the lure of the fabled peaks endured, enticing others into the morass of muskeg and burned timber that might lead, eventually, to Athabasca Pass.

First into the fray was Walter Wilcox, who, in 1896, with R.L. Barrett, and guides Fred Stephens and Tom Lusk, forged a route north from Lake Louise, across Bow Pass and Wilcox Pass to the Sunwapta Valley – roughly the route of today's Icefields Parkway. As they descended the Mistaya Valley, Stephens led the packstring through a forest fire. In the North Saskatchewan Valley, wind toppled Wilcox's camera on a summit, dashing it to pieces. Using a tool box carried for just such emergencies, the photographer managed to reassemble the apparatus. Members of the party were the first white men to glimpse the Saskatchewan Glacier and the Athabasca Glacier.

Three weeks out on the trail, the expedition duplicated Coleman's wrong turn of 1892. With greater zeal than that exhibited by Coleman, Wilcox

On trips in 1895 and 1896, Walter Wilcox helped to blaze the route north from Laggan. Bill Peyto — Wilcox's trail guide in 1895 — appears as a tiny dot in this view on the summit of Observation Peak, taken during its first ascent.

attempted to make the scenery around Fortress Lake fit the dream of Athabasca Pass. He invested a week in triangulating the peaks. The party rafted to the west end of the lake, where Wilcox and Barrett descended the Wood River a short distance, still hoping to find the well-concealed giants. Wilcox's candidate for Mt. Hooker looked promising, until he discovered a mistake in his computations: "... Mt. Hooker fell twenty-three hundred feet and came down to ten thousand five hundred feet never to rise again, and our enthusiasm fell with it." The party turned for home.

III. A New World at Our Feet

Any summit view reveals tantalizing glimpses of new terrain — the seeds that will germinate into future trips.

The cultivation comes in planning a journey to one or more of those peaks. The harvest is a successful ascent. But before the feast on a summit is over, a mountaineer's eyes wander, culling more seeds from the boundless furrows of peak and valley.

John Norman Collie was no stranger to summit views. English by birth, Scots and Irish by ancestry, Collie was among the mountaineering and the scientific elite of the late-Victorian era. He had climbed in Scotland, in the Alps, and in the Himalaya, often sharing the rope with the brilliant mountaineer, Alfred Mummery – the founder of modern alpinism. When Mummery disappeared on Nanga Parbat in 1895, Collie inherited the mantle as the world's greatest all-round mountaineer: adept at rock climbing, caving, alpine climbing, and

Coleman, Wilcox, Collie, and Stutfield weren't the only ones to thrash about in the woods in search of elusive mountains. Jean Habel (AHH-bull) was a German who first visited the Rockies in 1896. The following year he returned to try and find a peak that he had seen from the railway between Laggan and Field. In his quest, Habel failed to find his "Hidden Mountain," but was able to claim the "discoveries" of Takakkaw Falls and Twin Falls. He was the first mountaineer to take steps on the Wapta Icefield, ascending the Yoho Glacier a few days before Collie's party used Bow Glacier to approach Mt. Gordon. Habel returned to the Rockies in 1901, when he journeyed to the head of the Athabasca Valley and became the first to photograph Mt. Columbia and its neighbouring peaks from the north. Habel was planning to return to the Rockies in 1902 — he apparently corresponded with Collie regarding approaches to the icefield peaks. This would have made it a three-party race for Mt. Columbia. But Habel did not make the trip and died soon after.

expeditions. As a professor of chemistry at University College in London, Collie was on the team that first investigated the inert gases. He claimed to have discovered neon – although official credit went to two others. He made the first neon lamp and proposed a dynamic structure for benzene. Collie was a pioneer in colour photography, and in 1896 took the first X-ray photograph used in diagnostic medicine.

After his visit in 1897, Collie was smitten by the Canadian Rockies. He would later call them "the most beautiful mountain country I know of." The rugged, glacier-worn landscape mirrored the crags and corries of his Scottish stomping grounds. But there was spice in the measure beyond nostalgia – the Rockies were relatively unknown and unexplored. When on Mt. Lefroy's summit, Collie studied neighbouring Mt. Victoria. He led its first ascent two days later. From Mt. Victoria, Collie set his sights on Mt. Balfour, a glacier-clad peak some 20 kilometres north. In the attempt to climb Mt. Balfour, his party reached the summit of Mt. Gordon, where he saw another peak towering on the northwestern skyline. Leaving the more southerly peaks – including the much coveted, Mt. Assiniboine – to others, Collie again struck north in August 1897, and with George Baker and Peter Sarbach, made the first ascent of Mt. Sarbach, and the first attempts on Mt. Freshfield and Mt. Forbes. Although he knew that A.P. Coleman had unseated Mt. Brown, the view north from the slopes of Mt. Freshfield had included a magnificent, lofty, snow-covered mountain. Against his

Jean Habel's 1901 photograph of Mt. Columbia from the north

better judgement, Collie succumbed to the hope that the mythic Mt. Hooker might still lurk three week's travel from Laggan.

Although Collie planned to spend the summer of 1898 in the Alps, during the winter of 1897-98 he read all that he could find about exploration of the Rockies. He chanced upon the report of the Palliser Expedition, which had explored western Canada from 1857 to 1860. Of principal interest to Collie was the account of James Hector, doctor and geologist to the expedition. Hector had traversed the Bow, Mistaya, and North Saskatchewan valleys, and had named many features. Hector claimed that the peak he named Mt. Murchison – somewhere along the upper North Saskatchewan River – was the highest

mountain in the Rockies. Collie wondered: Could Hector have been referring to Mt. Forbes? And could Mt. Forbes be the Mt. Hooker of David Douglas? And what was the fine snowy peak that Collie had seen from Mt. Freshfield? (See Prologue.)

The summer of 1898 would be the first when competition stoked the fires of exploration in the Rockies. From correspondence the previous winter with Charles Thompson, Collie became aware that members of the Appalachian Mountain Club were planning trips to the Canadian mountains. This much was true, but Collie got some of the details wrong. He thought that Charles Fay was planning to attempt Mt. Forbes. But what Fay and Thompson were planning, in separate parties

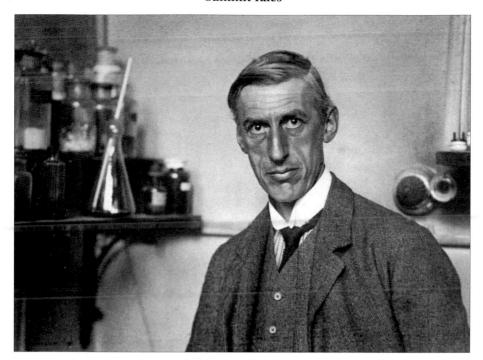

"If he was a great scientist, he was no less a gifted artist, an aesthetc in the finest sense, a romantic-minded Celt, and a robust athlete never out of training. His accomplishments were many, and he lived, almost literally, for beauty." From John Norman Collie's obituary in the 1942-43 *Canadian Alpine Journal*, by Geoffrey Winthrop Young

and by different routes, were renewed attempts on Mt. Balfour. In a letter to Thompson in March 1898, Collie provided his American friend with details of approaches to the northerly peaks while taking a jab at Fay: "I don't know about mountaineering etiquette out in America, but over on this side of the duck pond it would have been considered the right thing to first write Baker or me to find out what we intended to do...."

No copy of Thompson's reply exists, but in May, Collie wrote to tell Thompson that he was abandoning his plans for the Alps: "...we shall ascend or descend on the Canadian Rockies at the end of July if all goes well. My programme is an ambitious one. [Mt.] Murchison from the Pipestone [Valley]

to begin with, then [Mt.] Forbes, and then we shall force our way north to [Mt.] Brown and [Mt.] Hooker...."

Collie's party would include Hugh Stutfield and Hermann Woolley, both experienced alpinists. But there would be no Swiss mountain guide. Collie was accustomed to climbing without one, and, although Stutfield and Woolley were both men of means, the expense of travelling from Britain precluded importing another person from the Continent.

With Bill Peyto (PEE-toe) as trail guide, the party left Laggan on July 31. Compared to present day outings, this seems late, but the mountaineers of the late 19th Century lived at the wane of the Little Ice Age, when the winter snowpack was three to four times that

Explorers knew the three rivers that combine near today's Saskatchewan River Crossing as the North Fork (North Saskatchewan), the Middle Fork (Howse), and the Little Fork (Mistaya). Heading north, most outfitters would choose to ford the Little Fork, and then try to cross the Middle Fork upstream from its confluence with the North Fork. This trick reduced the water hazard, sometimes to manageable levels. But in this view taken in the early 1900s, the southbound packstring is crossing the North Saskatchewan River below the confluence with the Middle Fork. Guides, outfitters, and clients called this "the big swim."

characteristic of the early 21st Century. Snow choked the high passes until early August; the rivers, charged with snowmelt, were uncrossable before then.

Because James Hector had mentioned that Mt. Murchison was visible from Pipestone Pass, Collie's party followed the Pipestone Valley north from Laggan. A few days out on the trail, Collie became aware that Hector had been wrong – the view from Pipestone Pass included no peak as high as Mt. Murchison was reported to be. The expe-

dition descended the Siffleur Valley to the North Saskatchewan Valley. They had been on the trail a week and had accomplished no mountaineering.

The North Saskatchewan River posed a monumental barrier to explorers. A.P. Coleman had rafted it in 1892, and had used a collapsible canvas boat to cross it the following year. Peyto wisely led Collie's party upstream to where the river gathered from its three forks. By fording two of the forks – the Mistaya River and the Howse River

– and then heading upstream along the main stem of the North Saskatchewan, Peyto was able to reduce the risk to his party. When asked about the potential peril, Peyto laconically commented that if a rider fell from his horse into a river, he should be able to pick his way to shore, unless in the process he struck his head on a rock, whereupon he "would die easily." No one in Collie's party went for a swim, but along the way, various horses dunked their packboxes, half-ruining the party's supplies of bacon, flour, and sugar.

On August 11, while Peyto and his men scouted and chopped trail, Collie and Stutfield made the first ascent of a lowly mountain, from which Collie carried on the survey work begun by Baker the previous year. (See Prologue.) The mountain later became known as Survey Peak. On the same day, Charles Thompson's party made the first ascent of Mt. Balfour. This was probably the first time in the Rockies that two first ascents were made on the same day.

Back on the trail, Collie's party inched upvalley for a few days before Peyto reported that the route was impossible. Collie, who had not crossed an ocean and a continent to be turned back by mere muskeg, raging rivers, and fallen trees, dug into the party's stash of whisky to appease wild man Bill. Thus fortified, Peyto saddled up and forded to the east bank where the going was decidedly easier. The others followed. On August 17th, the expedition crested Sunwapta Pass to camp in the shadow of the "noble snow-crowned peak" known today as Mt. Athabasca.

It wasn't until after dinner that the men inventoried their food supply. "We knew that it was pretty low, as we had started with an insufficient stock, our appetites were healthy, and the dogs had eaten a great deal more of our bacon than was good either for them or for us; but we were quite unprepared for the alarming state of affairs which the inspection disclosed." The plan for tomorrow: Stutfield would hunt sheep; Collie and Woolley would climb the peak. It would be a rare day in the history of early mountaineering in the Rockies – a double success.

With Woolley leading Collie much of the way, the two climbers took a route on Mt. Athabasca that is seldom repeated – the icy, shattered, limestone spine of the northeast ridge. Ever-steepening to its conclusion, the route butted into an overhanging step, just beneath the summit. "After what we had gone through down below, fifteen feet, even though it did overhang, was not going to keep us from the top. How it was surmounted I have forgotten, but I remember how we saw the summit almost within a stone's-throw of us, and how at 5:15 PM we stepped on to it."

"The view that lay before us in the evening light was one that does not often fall to the lot of modern mountaineers. A new world was spread at our feet; to the westward stretched a vast ice-field probably never before seen by human eye, and surrounded by entirely unknown, unnamed and unclimbed peaks." Collie and Woolley were looking at the Columbia Icefield. It was typical of his era that Collie gave no credit to the possible experiences of First Nations, but in appraising that remarkable view, he revealed a grasp of the landscape that can only be called visionary. Intuitively, Collie identified the tri-oceanic divide on the crest of the icefield, from which waters flow to the Arctic, Atlantic, and Pacific oceans. He gave names to six mountains, including a peak named for David Douglas, since renamed Mt. Kitchener.

Collie took stock of the sea of unclimbed peaks spread out into the distance: "... I at once recognized the great peak I was in search of; moreover a short distance to the north-east of this mountain, another, almost as high, also flat-topped, but ringed round with sheer precipices, reared its head into the sky above all its fellows. At once I concluded that these might be the two lost mountains, Brown and Hooker." Today they are known, respectively, as Mt. Columbia and Mt. Alberta.

Collie spent an hour and fifteen minutes surveying on the summit, while Woolley shivered beside him, his eye on the pocketwatch. The pair took a different route down, stumbling into camp at 11:00 PM. Peyto and his men had been anxious, but Stutfield told them "that when they got used to the ways of climbers they would cease to feel alarmed when a party did not show up for dinner." And there was dinner that night. On the hunt in Wilcox Pass, Stutfield and the cook, Nigel Vavasour, had killed three bighorn sheep.

Two days later, the party ascended Athabasca Glacier to make an attempt

Fellow explorer, Mary Schäffer, took this photograph of A.P. Coleman near Wilcox Pass during a chance meeting in 1907. Coleman was on his way to make the first attempt on Mt. Robson.

Left: When botanist David Douglas went collecting in western Canada in 1827, he initiated a controversy, the echoes of which reverberate almost two centuries later. Whether Douglas blundered, fudged, or outright lied about the "Titans of Athabasca Pass" is immaterial. In making his description of monumental mountains he dangled an irresistible carrot for mountaineers, who readily took the bait.

on what they thought was Mt. Brown (Mt. Columbia). After nine hours of threading around crevasses and plodding through the snow with thunder threatening, Collie, Stutfield, and Woolley gave up the attempt, settling instead for the first ascent of Snow Dome. The views that day did not support Collie's earlier speculation that they had found Mt. Hooker and Mt. Brown. The climbers could detect no pass between the two candidate peaks "by which any animal less active than a [mountain] goat could cross." Stutfield commented that "the solution of the problem was, in fact, as far off as ever."

Leaving the camp in Sunwapta Pass, Peyto and the climbers spent the next week exploring down the Sunwapta Valley, where they hoped to "find the Athabasca Pass and the lost [Committee] Punch Bowl." They found nothing of the sort, but Collie, Stutfield, and Woolley made the first ascent of Diadem Peak. After returning to Sunwapta Pass the climbers discovered that "some of the mutton had gone bad in our absence, so we decided to make tracks homewards without further delay." On the way, the dogs polished off the bread and the bacon. Food was so scarce, the climbers were certain that the cook was serving "the uppers of Bill Peyto's boots, which had recently shown signs of disintegration." Hungry or not, the climbers made the first attempt on Mt. Murchison, and the first ascent of Mt. Thompson.

The following winter, back in London, Collie found and read a copy

George Baker takes a break while on the way down from the first ascent of Mt. Jimmy Simpson in 1897. Smoke from forest fires, not from Baker's pipe, clouds the view.

of the journal of David Douglas. He concluded that: "If Douglas climbed a 17,000 [Collie meant 16,000] feet peak alone on a May afternoon, when the snow must have been pretty deep on the ground, all one can say is that he must have been an uncommonly active person. What, of course, he really did was to ascend the Mount Brown of Professor Coleman, which is about 9000 feet high. These two fabulous Titans, therefore, which for nearly seventy years have been masquerading as the monarchs of the Canadian Rockies, must now finally be deposed; and Mounts Forbes, Columbia and Alberta, with Peak Robson, west of Yellowhead Pass, must reign in their stead." (Collie authored *Climbing on the Himalaya and Other Mountain Ranges* in 1902. In

a curious anecdote to history, the publisher of the book was a Scottish company named David Douglas.)

In 1925, American mountaineer, J. Monroe Thorington – the foremost detective of Rocky Mountain history – concluded that Douglas, who left two contradictory accounts of his climb, had greatly enhanced his descriptions of the two mountains, and had assigned names and elevations *after* his return to England. Douglas had also embraced what Thorington called "the tradition of height." Although no one had ever formally surveyed the elevation of Athabasca Pass, most everyone involved in the fur trade thought that it was 11,000 feet above sea level. (Its elevation is 5736 feet.) The vaulted heights that Douglas bestowed on Mt.

Hooker and Mt. Brown were clearly an expression of alpine flattery – the academics for whom he named the peaks received the maximum return for supporting his collecting expedition. What Douglas would never know was that his mistake accelerated the exploration of the Rockies in a way that saw more ground covered in a few years than might otherwise have been opened up in decades.

IV. THE MOUNTAINS FOR THE TREES

THE EXPEDITION OF 1898 had often been only a meal or a mountain shy of failure, but Collie and Stutfield were not yet done with fiasco. In 1900, coveting more than ever the great peaks that rim the western and northern fringes of the Columbia Icefield, they embarked on a journey through country so challenging as to extract every shred of perseverance. Their logic was simple: Athabasca Pass was closer to points on the Canadian Pacific Railway north of Golden, BC, than it was to Laggan. A.P. Coleman did not publish an account of his 1891 Columbia River trip until 1911, so Collie and Stutfield might be forgiven a certain ignorance of what they were biting off to chew when they decided to approach Mt. Columbia and Mt. Bryce by a similar route.

The expedition was fraught with mishap from the very first steps when a horse pitched over onto the party's axe man, injuring him so badly that he had to be packed off to hospital in Banff on the next train. Soon after leaving the railway station at Donald, the men descended into a green hell. Stutfield described the visual experience: "It is hard to convey in words the impressions left on one's mind by a journey through the underworld of these great forests, where the sunlight hardly penetrates and the massy leafage forms a canopy overhead that screens all view of the outside world. For days together we journeyed without so much as catching a glimpse of the surrounding mountains, and all we could see of the sky was an occasional bit of blue peeping through the narrow openings here and there." Collie described the auditory experience: "... the chopping of the axe and the drip of water from the leaves are the only sounds unless unprintable language is suddenly hurled at some wretched pack animal." Fred Stephens, packer on the trip, thought that the conditions were the worst he had ever encountered, adding: "... it was raining 7 days out of 6, to make it more pleasant." After three weeks of toil, during which they covered less than 80 kilometres, Collie and Stutfield clambered from the verdant depths along the Bush River to lowly summits and found themselves 25 kilometres shy of Mt. Columbia and Mt. Bryce. The following day, the food ran out.

Neither mountaineer ever openly regretted the summer of 1900, but others collectively scratched their heads. In September of that year, Charles Noyes of the AMC wrote to Charles Thompson, who earlier that summer had ascended the Alexandra Valley with the hope of meeting Collie near Mt. Bryce. "It is a great pity that Collie lost his summer scrambling about those steeps and thickets... What was Collie's plan and idea? With so much splendid country to work up and peaks to master by his tried approach up the Bow [Valley], how could he throw away time by starting from a route that promised such odds against him?" Two summers later, Collie and Stutfield may well have been asking themselves the same questions, for the men who had paid such great dues would find themselves two weeks late in the race for Mt. Columbia's crown.

Great Expectations

Edward Whymper was a witness to the most celebrated fall in mountaineering history. In 1865, as his party descended from the first ascent of the Matterhorn, one man stumbled, causing the rope to break between Whymper and the four climbers ahead of him. In horror, Whymper and his companions watched as the four, including one of Switzerland's celebrated mountain guides, plunged to their deaths.

Whymper had risen to prominence as an alpinist near the end of the Golden Age of European mountaineering, when all of the continent's principal peaks – and many of the lesser ones – were first climbed. The first ascent of the Matterhorn was the crowning achievement of Whymper's meteoric career – he was only 25 years old. But the tragedy of the descent would haunt him for the rest of his days.

An Englishman, Whymper was a talented engraver who harbored a life-long desire to be an Arctic explorer. In the early part of his career, he made his living from selling woodcut prints of alpine views; initially of the Alps, but later of Greenland and the Andes. When photography eclipsed engraving as a means of illustration, Whymper relied on public speaking and writing to pay for his explorations. His *Scrambles Among the Alps*, published in 1871, was for a century considered the greatest mountaineering work. In the 1890s, he released the classic study of the

---

Opposite: Surveyor George Dawson brought Mt. Assiniboine to the attention of the world in 1884. In 1895, Charles Fay of the Appalachian Mountain Club viewed the distant peak from the upper slopes of Mt. Stephen, and wondered: "Who will be its Whymper, and when?"

Above: Whymper was sincere in his desire to provide the CPR with detailed information. He annotated his photographs, such as this 1901 panorama from Isolated Peak, with many observations.

"There have been joys too great to be described in words, and there have been griefs upon which I have not dared to dwell; and with these in mind I say: Climb if you will, but remember that courage and strength are naught without prudence, and that a momentary negligence may destroy the happiness of a lifetime. Do nothing in haste; look well to each step; and from the beginning think what may be the end." Edward Whymper, *Scrambles Amongst the Alps*, 1871

Andes, and guidebooks to two of Europe's mountaineering centres: Chamonix and Zermatt.

Whymper was probably looking for new terrain to explore and to write about when the Canadian Pacific Railway (CPR) approached him in 1900 at the conclusion of a speaking tour of the United States. The railway company, eager to pack visitors into its ensemble of mountain hotels, wanted to promote the Rockies as a new playground for mountain-lovers from Europe. Who better to help publicize the "Canadian Alps" than the man whom the public associated with the European Alps?

At the CPR's invitation, Whymper

rode in luxury along the rails from Montréal to Vancouver and back that same year. The following summer, he descended on the Rockies with much fanfare and a contingent of four Swiss mountain guides. The railway company expected him to make suggestions for laying out trail systems, and for developing its facilities in the mountains. Many, including some higher-ups in the CPR, also expected Whymper to make the first ascent of Mt. Assiniboine (11,870 feet/3618 metres), the "Canadian Matterhorn" and sixth highest peak in the Rockies.

But Whymper, then 61, had no such high intent. When asked if he would

Whymper generated masses of material during his first visit to the Rockies. This view shows three of his guides descending from the first ascent of Mt. Collie in 1901, with the climbing route overlaid.

attempt Mt. Assiniboine, he replied: "Not so. A man does not climb mountains like Assiniboine after he is sixty years old." The frustration of his mountain guides exacerbated this misunderstanding between Whymper and his employer. The guides were among the elite of their profession but soon found themselves under-worked. During their first two months in the Rockies, they made only five ascents. Poor weather played a part in this, but Whymper was often preoccupied with photography, exploring for minerals, and keeping meticulous records of weather and elevations. The proud guides, resentful of their roles as glorified porters,

complained. One of the guides – Christian Klucker – sarcastically professed that his principal accomplishment in 1901 was "to climb a tree in the primeval forest, to see where on earth we were." Whymper criticized the guides roundly in return, stating that they should be paid less and work more.

The "conqueror of the Matterhorn," accustomed to being treated as a celebrity, found few in the Canadian west who would give him an inch for his fame, or for his 28 pieces of luggage. He responded by treating all in a high-handed manner. His capacity for drink worsened matters. Ralph Campbell, who packed supplies for Whymper,

reported that the mountaineer's "daily allowance was one bottle of House of Commons Scotch and ten pints of ale." Campbell added that when he had been in Whymper's hotel rooms he had never seen Whymper "farther from a Scotch and soda than the length of his arm."

The catalogue of people that Whymper alienated in 1901 included his trail guide and outfitter, Bill Peyto, a man with a reputation for answering to no one. After setting up Whymper's camp in the Little Yoho Valley in early August, Peyto – using lame horses as an excuse – deserted, leaving Whymper in chaos in the backcountry. The outraged mountaineer stormed back to Field to find a replacement, where he chanced to meet a young climber, James Outram (OOT-rum), who was fresh from the first ascents of two lofty summits – Chancellor Peak and Mt. Vaux (VOX).

Whymper's summer of 1901 would have been a complete publicity bust for

the CPR had this encounter not taken place. Whymper invited Outram to join his party. Outram, a minister from Ipswich, England, and a mountaineer with experience in the Alps, had come to Canada the previous year to combat the effects of a nervous breakdown. In his own account, *In the Heart of the Canadian Rockies*, published in 1905, Outram painted a glowing picture of Whymper's generosity. But it seems more likely that the upstart mountaineer, seeing the opportunity presented by a well-equipped camp and the four disgruntled mountain guides, seized the moment to make mountaineering hay.

Sometimes in the company of Whymper, but more often with only the guides, Outram stormed the peaks north of Emerald Lake, making ten first ascents in two weeks. Outram concluded the itinerary with the first crossing of Balfour Pass, when he and two of the guides walked from the Yoho

Opposite: Bill Peyto and Whymper's mountain guides conspired to create this irreverent trailside memorial to the conqueror of the Matterhorn. One of the labels reads: "Remains of E. Whymper."

Left: James Outram took this photo of his guides, Christian Bohren and Christian Häsler, just before they reached the summit of Mt. Assiniboine in 1901.

Valley to the Chalet at Lake Louise, covering 35 kilometres, half of it off-trail, in 12 hours.

Perhaps to goad the elder mountaineer, Bill Peyto had returned to the Yoho camp to inform Whymper that the summit of "Canada's Matterhorn" yet awaited a climber worthy of the attempt. The mountain had eluded Walter Wilcox for the third time earlier in the summer. During all previous forays, parties had required at least three days from Banff to reach the base of the peak. Peyto boasted that he could lead a party there in two days, and return in less, and that anybody interested in climbing the mountain ought to get to it, as summer was just about over.

Whymper did not take the bait, but Outram, sensing that a five-day expedition was within his means, agreed. After his trek to Lake Louise, and after making the first ascent of Cathedral Mountain with two of Whymper's guides on August 26, Outram boarded the train to Banff, where Peyto was secretly assembling the expedition. Outram brought with him two of the CPR's mountain guides from Field, Christian Kaufmann and Christian Bohrer, to better ensure success. The party set out for Mt. Assiniboine on August 31, and made their first attempt on the peak two days later. The day began favourably, but mists soon gathered. In the poor visibility, Outram and the guides reached the top of Lunette Peak, the southerly summit of Mt. Assiniboine. The following day, in perfect weather, the trio made the first ascent and traverse of Mt. Assiniboine. The next day, snow blanketed the peaks and the valleys. In an epic forced march, Peyto led the triumphant party through the early blizzard back to Banff, delivering them just five days and five hours after they had left town.

James Outram was the star of the Rockies in the summer of 1901. Whymper subsequently disappeared,

Whymper's four mountain guides pose for James Outram on the summit of Mt. Habel (now known as Mont des Poilus), on the occasion of its first ascent, August 1901.

spending most of the autumn exploring alone in the remote Ice River Valley. His official report to the CPR, penned in January 1902, was largely a lament of his supplies, his equipment, and his relations with his employer and the Swiss guides. From the railway company's point of view, the document was virtually a waste of money. However, the CPR did implement a few of Whymper's recommendations concerning trail development in Yoho and near Lake Louise, and it embraced his slogan that the Rockies were "fifty Switzerlands in one."

Whymper was itching to return in 1902, but the CPR politely told him "no." In 1903, he arrived in Montréal, wanting to walk along the railway line from the east side of the Rockies to the Fraser Canyon. The CPR had more practical plans to employ him around Lake Louise and Moraine Lake, and in the Crowsnest Pass. Whymper scoffed at this, and set off on his bizarre walk along the rails. Ever attendant to detail, he recorded crossing 456 bridges – a nugget of dubious promotional value to the CPR, which already knew how many bridges spanned the rivers, streams, and canyons along its mainline.

Whymper was able to milk one more junket out of the CPR in 1904, but his accomplishments were trivial. When he returned uninvited in 1905, the railway company bluntly told him that it no longer needed his services. He auctioned off the equipment that he had cached at Field, taking a considerable loss. In 1909, Whymper visited the Rockies for the last time, as a guest at the Alpine Club of Canada's annual camp at Lake O'Hara. Piqued that other British mountaineers had also been invited, he stayed at the camp for but three of its nine days duration, never cracking a smile. He was back in England five weeks after he had departed for Canada. Whymper died at Chamonix two years later, aged 71. Mt. Whymper, near Vermilion Pass in Kootenay National Park, commemorates the man of whom many had expectations, but whose greatness as a mountaineer was already a thing long tarnished.

In making the first ascent and traverse of Mt. Assiniboine in 1901, James Outram and his guides got it backwards. They ascended the relatively easy southwest face, and descended the much more difficult northeast arête, opposite to the way most climbers traverse the peak today. Outram took this photo of the summit at the beginning of the descent.

Full of Peaks and Glory

Despite his enthusiasm for alpine glory, the truth was that John Norman Collie repeatedly returned bushed and frustrated from his trips in the Canadian wilds. In his first three summers in the Rockies, the world's greatest mountaineer had managed only 11 summits, two of which were day-trips from the Chalet at Lake Louise. Reeling from the Bush River adventure, Collie chose to climb in the relative civilization of Norway's Lofoten Islands in the summer of 1901. During the following winter, he planned an expedition to the Rockies that he hoped would set matters right. But as is so often the case with those who lay the groundwork, little of the alpine glory claimed in the summer of 1902 would be his.

Buoyed by his successes in 1901, James Outram also had designs on the big icefield peaks north of Laggan. From the summits of Mt. Habel and Mt. Collie, Outram had gazed longingly to the north, where the preposterous, isolated fang of Mt. Forbes loomed on the horizon. Outram knew that he could hire a trail guide and a mountain guide to get him to the general area of the peak, but he would enjoy a greater chance of success by tapping Collie's firsthand knowledge of the headwaters of the North Saskatchewan River.

Accordingly, Outram wrote Collie to suggest that the pair combine forces. The proposal clearly rankled and perplexed Collie, who broached the matter in a letter to Charles Thompson in

Opposite: "Owing to the steepness of the rocks, some hours elapsed before a convenient breakfast-place presented itself; and by the time we found one we were all pretty hungry." Collie took the photograph high on Mt. Forbes during the first ascent.

Above: Trail guides used smoldering campfires, called smudges, to help keep the bugs down at campsites. They often lit smudges for the benefit of the horses, too. Collie, wearing the white hat, is central in this picture from 1902. Stutfield is to the left, with Woolley or Weed in the tent. Hans Kaufmann is on the right.

Of the two surviving photographs that can be identified as being taken on the summit of Mt. Forbes in 1902, one shows the backsides of seven men peering over the summit cornice. This more interesting view shows the cornice, with the view north through firesmoke, to Mt. Erasmus.

March 1902. "We shall probably go for the Freshfield Group and Forbes and later work north to Columbia. It is going to be purely a climbing trip and we shall try to keep as may 'scalps' away from Outram as we can...." Collie's climbing companions would be fellow Brits, Hugh Stutfield, Hermann Woolley, and George Weed, with the mountain guide, Hans Kaufmann, who was stationed in Canada.

Hindsight reveals that Collie's jealous ambition got the better of him. Rather than "guarding" access to the icefield peaks, he should have agreed to team with his competitor. What Collie conceded to do was to meet Outram on a specified date, to attempt Mt. Forbes. Outram saw his opportunity – the field was thrown open. With Hans Kaufmann's brother, Christian, as mountain guide, and Bill Peyto, Jimmy Simpson, and Fred Ballard – the most

adept trio ever to pack horses and blaze trail in the Rockies – Outram departed Laggan on July 9, 1902, a week before Collie arrived in Canada.

Many blessings flowed from Outram's success on Mt. Assiniboine in 1901. The Canadian Pacific Railway donated the services of Kaufmann for the entire summer of 1902. Edouard Deville, the Surveyor General of Canada, contributed a transit and a tripod to the expedition. Two cameras, 480 photographic plates, three barometers, field glasses, maps, clinometers, thermometers, four ice axes, an air mattress, and various other "semi-scientific" instruments "formed a most harassing climax to the number of packs" that Peyto loaded onto ten horses.

Outram's party was so well requisitioned it would finish its two-month long expedition with rations to spare. Peyto departed from the outbound leg

The combined parties of Collie and Outram take a break on Freshfield Glacier on August 4, 1902. Christian Kaufmann is on the right, with his brother, Hans, beside him. Hugh Stutfield is in the centre. Collie is seated, second from the left. James Outram is between Stutfield and Collie. Jack Robson took the photo: this was his first time walking on a glacier.

of the trip after he had cached supplies at the mouth of the Mistaya River in a trapping cabin used by Simpson and Ballard in the off-season. On the way north, Peyto's string had leap-frogged with that of outfitter Fred Stephens, who was packing supplies in advance of Collie's arrival.

No matter how you read the accounts of the summer of 1902 – Stutfield, Outram, and Collie each left versions   Outram's intent seems clear. Just ten days out from Laggan, the first peak that he and Christian Kaufmann attempted and climbed was Mt. Columbia (12,294 feet/3747 metres), second highest in the Rockies. Five days later, the pair climbed the highest of the five summits of Mt. Lyell (lie-ELL). After that, they trooped up the mountain now known as Mons Peak. Outram returned to the cabin at the mouth of the Mistaya River and pinned a note

for Collie on the door – "Meet you at Glacier Lake" – or something to that effect. He had a lot of nerve. Although Mt. Forbes and Mt. Murchison remained unclimbed, the ex-vicar had stolen John Norman Collie's thunder.

George Weed, who accompanied Collie in 1902, wrote to Charles Thompson after the expedition: "Of course it was a disappointment, although Collie would scarcely give it expression, that Outram was picking the plums that ought to have gone to Collie... I may do Outram an injustice, but his conduct seemed to me to suggest the thought that he was getting what mountains he could alone and trying to share all others with us... [he] made all sorts of suggestions looking toward keeping our company and to find out our future plans...." Although no one put the thought in print, what was most disturbing to the other mountaineers was

After some wrong-headed routefinding in the approach valley, Collie's party split into two ropes to begin the ascent of the west glacier of Howse Peak. Hans Kaufmann led the first rope. Collie took the photograph.

that they could not equate Outram's behaviour with the fact that he was a minister.

It appears that even Outram later experienced misgivings, although he did not apologize. His account, given in his 1905 book, *In the Heart of the Canadian Rockies*, muddled the sequence of his ascents, chronicling those of Mt. Columbia and Mt. Lyell *after* he described his climbs with Collie's party on Mt. Freshfield and Mt. Forbes. To the casual reader of his day, this might have given the impression that the two parties agreed to climb Mt. Freshfield and Mt. Forbes together, after which Collie went home, leaving the greatest prize – Mt. Columbia – to Outram. This, of course, had not been the case.

Although Outram's methods and his respect for the mountaineering etiquette of the late-Victorian era were flawed, his and Christian Kaufmann's climbing was without peer. The first ascent of Mt. Columbia was an endurance test, the likes of which had not been seen in the Rockies – a marathon snow plod, requiring thirteen hours from camp in Castleguard Meadows to the summit, and nine hours for the

"An hour or two's work next morning sufficed to bring the raft to completion. It was a large and very fine specimen of naval architecture, made of good-sized logs lashed together with cinches (pack-ropes), and wooden cross-pieces and branches laid thereon to raise our goodly pile of baggage above the water. She was named "The Glacier Belle," but we had no liquor to waste on her christening." Collie's party used the raft to bypass a forest fire on the north shore of Glacier Lake. When they returned to the craft a few days later, the logs had soaked up so much water, most of the precious freeboard was gone. Collie, readily identified by the white hat that he often wore in 1902, sits atop the pile of gear. Hans Kaufmann is to the right.

"What is there left to say of Mt. Forbes — that wonderful mountain we had placed, with some temerity, at the end of our climbing programme? It is a height to which one may look up, as if Kim to the rim of the Himalaya, and say, 'Surely the Gods live here.' Skyward rearing, like a watchtower of the immortals, it is a perpetual challenge."

J. Monroe Thorington, "Climbs in the Forbes-Lyell and Other Groups of the Canadian Rockies, 1926", *American Alpine Journal*, 1926

"...[Mt.] Forbes is much more beautiful at a distance than when you are actually standing on him....

"We, less energetic, preferred to take a brief rest after our labours [of climbing Mt. Forbes]. Yet we were not altogether idle; for Woolley, who seems as he grows older to get more enterprising than ever, climbed up on the slopes of Coronation Peak with his big camera, and took some admirable photographs of Mount Forbes." [August 12, 1902]

Hugh Stutfield, *Climbs and Exploration in the Canadian Rockies*, 1903, (both quotes)

return. The first ascent of Mt. Bryce by its challenging northeast ridge was, hands down, the boldest climb made in the Rockies until the first ascent of Mt. Robson in 1913. The route is still considered a test piece. Outram and Kaufmann added spice by downclimbing the crux in the dark – a 20 metre cliff, higher than their rope was long. The duo completed their triumph at the headwaters of the North Saskatchewan River with the first ascent of Mt. Wilson, traversing the icefield that drapes the massive mountain, from north to south.

Fortune smiled on Outram and Kaufmann for the duration of their 54-day outing. Neither of them fell into a crevasse, which for a rope of only two climbers would have meant certain disaster. Including the two peaks climbed with Collie's party, the pair made ten first ascents – all of them over 10,000 feet, two over 11,000 feet, and one over 12,000 feet. Remarkably, in every case but one, the successful ascents were accomplished on the first attempt.

Collie's party arrived at the mouth of the Mistaya River on July 27. There they found Outram's note, but of greater importance to Collie was the location of two bottles – one of whisky, the

Some modern day mountaineers have disputed when the first ascent of Mt. Murchison was accomplished, but this photo is proof-positive that Collie's party reached the north summit in 1902. The south summit, which may be a few metres higher, is central in the view.

other of brandy – that he had stashed at the base of a tree on his prior visit, in 1898. Although Collie had told outfitters Fred Stephens and Bill Peyto of the bottles' location, neither man had found them, but not for want of trying. "The ground looked as though bears or wild boars had been rooting round; but the men had dug at the foot of every tree but the right one, across which another trunk had fallen, covering the white stone and the burial-place of the bottles."

Fred Stephens was reluctant to take his outfit across the raging Mistaya River, so Collie's party elected to make

a reconnaissance of Mt. Murchison, whose true summit they expected was a good distance east. They were pleasantly surprised to find that it was a relatively straightforward, if long, ascent to one of the mountain's two high points, and that James Outram had not visited it. At 4:00 PM on July 29, the four men clambered onto the corniced summit ridge of what was once thought to be the highest mountain in the Rockies. "A very brief examination of our barometers showed that Mount Murchison would have to suffer the degradation which, sooner of later, is the lot of most mountains in this region... So far

As he had done on Mt. Freshfield in 1897, Collie called off the ascent of Mt. Lyell in 1902 to carry out survey work. In both cases, the guides were outraged. Two first ascents went by the boards so that the climbers could fill more blanks on the map.

from its being 15,781 feet, or 13,500 as [James] Hector imagined, Collie's Watkin barometer... only made it 11,300 feet above sea-level...." Mt. Murchison is 10,936 feet (3333 metres) high, and is not among the 50-highest peaks in the Canadian Rockies.

Next day, Stephens judged the Mistaya River sufficiently lower in volume and led his group across. In the evening, Collie and packer Jack Robson forded the Howse River on horseback to ride to Outram's camp at Glacier Lake. Outram was upvalley with Christian Kaufmann on Mons Peak. Thus snubbed, Collie and Robson returned but missed the fording place. The river pinned them in a hole, and in their efforts to escape, horses and riders swam separately for the bank.

Collie's party spent a day moving up the Howse Valley and along Freshfield Creek to be within striking distance of the southeast flank of Mt. Forbes. Outram's contingent arrived soon after camp was set up. Although Collie was outwardly polite, he must have been inwardly furious when Outram informed him that Mt. Columbia and Mt. Lyell had fallen. In his account, Stutfield glossed over the disappointment, even so far as to distort the purpose of the expedition. "Our chief ambition on this trip was to reach the summit of Mount Forbes...." At least in print, Mt. Columbia was never mentioned again.

From the camp, the climbers glassed Mt. Forbes. Their proposed route would be mostly on rock, but fresh snow covered the ledges and

Jimmy Simpson, trail guide to the glacier country

ridges on the upper part of the peak. Hoping that warm weather would clear the hazard, the combined teams turned their attention to the southwest and made the first ascent of Mt. Freshfield on August 4.

Favourable weather brought Mt. Forbes into condition. The ascent on August 10 was novel for any peak in the Rockies. It was the first time that climbers made a bivouac – a tent-less, high camp to shorten the approach to the climbing next day. Bivouacking went against the tradition of the Swiss guides, who were accustomed to climbing from the comfort of huts in Europe, and for most of whom, even camp life with the shelter of a tent was barely tolerable.

The route on Mt. Forbes was steep. Friable rock added danger to the diffi-culty. Woolley stated that, "The narrow crest of the ridge seemed to be held together only by the snow frozen against its sides...." High on the mountain, a large rock shot out from under the feet of Hans Kaufmann, who was first on a rope of three. The guide grabbed the crest of the ridge with his right hand, averting a fall that might have pulled Stutfield and Woolley from their stances. Nine hours after leaving their bivouac, the seven climbers staggered onto the tiny summit. The view was marvelous, tainted only by the disappointment – as evidenced by their barometers – that Mt. Forbes, too, would have to come down in standing. At 11,852 feet (3612 metres), it is the seventh highest peak in the Rockies.

After the two successful ascents,

Outram invited Collie to join him for an attempt on Mt. Bryce. This was salting the wound for Collie, who had spent the summer of 1900 groping through the greenery just trying to find the mountain. He declined. From that point, Outram's summer remained meteoric, while Collie's sparked, sputtered, and fizzled.

Outram soon departed for the head of the Alexandra River, and from there he and Christian Kaufmann climbed Mt. Bryce. Collie's party moved to Howse Pass. After making the first ascent of Howse Peak by its relatively easy west slopes, they beat along familiar trails to Glacier Lake, at the head of which they hoped to establish a basecamp to climb Mt. Lyell. But a forest fire that probably originated at Outram's earlier camp raged along the north shore. (This was the second time that Outram's party had torched a forest in three weeks.) While the packers and trail guides spent the better part of two days building a raft, the climbers – except for Stutfield who went goat hunting – remained in camp.

Beyond Glacier Lake, Collie and company ascended moraines to the Lyell Icefield. As the weather deteriorated, Collie called off the attempt on Mt. Lyell, preferring to ascend a knoll on the glacier in order to survey before the clouds rolled in. Hans Kaufmann was incensed. "What, not climb Mt. Lyell?... you will regret it very much!" After leaving the high point, the climbers descended the glacier and glissaded a steep snow slope. Collie bumped his pipe out of his mouth with his ice axe. He lunged for the pipe, lost his balance, and cartwheeled down the slope – the only fall recorded in his alpine climbing career.

Within three or four days travel of Collie's Glacier Lake camp, high, unclimbed mountains abounded – among them Mt. Wilson, Mt. Coleman, Cirrus Mountain, Mt. Amery, four of the summits of Mt. Lyell, and Mt. Saskatchewan. However, at this point in his account, Stutfield made an astonishing comment: "...it was decided that, as there appeared to be no more mountaineering of an interesting nature to be done in the neighbourhood, we should return with all speed to Laggan, and wind up the season with some climbing in the Valley of the Ten Peaks...." Although low on supplies, the party had enough to remain a few more days at the headwaters of the North Saskatchewan River. What probably prompted the exit was concern for the whereabouts of Outram, and the fear that, after having cleaned up the icefield peaks, he would move on to Laggan and knock off the two unclimbed giants of that neighbourhood – Deltaform Mountain and Hungabee Mountain. In fact, Outram's party was a week behind Collie's.

On their way to Laggan, Collie, Stutfield, Weed, and Woolley made the first ascent of Mt. Noyes, in the Mistaya Valley. The weather, which had been favourable for much of August, broke. After waiting five days at Moraine Lake for the skies to clear, Collie's party gave up on attempting Deltaform and Hungabee, which were out of condition. They settled for the first ascent of Neptuak Mountain on September 2. They enjoyed the climb, their last of that season, but Collie was clearly bitter over the summer of 1902. It would be eight years before he returned to the Canadian Rockies.

James Outram flashed in the pan. After making 28 first ascents in the Rockies in three summers – including five of the ten highest mountains summited to that point – he retired from climbing. He later became something of a statesman of Canadian mountaineering and a fixture at Alpine Club of Canada camps until his death in 1925.

The collective knowledge of several well-travelled, modern mountaineers has failed to place the location of this image, which shows Collie's party approaching a summit, probably in 1902.

Appointments with the King

I. A RUMOUR OF GREATNESS

TRAVELLERS HAVE BEEN NOTICING Mt. Robson for almost 200 years. The first reference to the mountain by name was in a diary entry by a fur trader in 1827. In 1898, James McEvoy of the Geological Survey of Canada crossed Yellowhead Pass. His report of that trip included the first published photograph of the mountain, and gave an estimate for Mt. Robson's height as 13,700 feet (4175 metres). The surveyor had apparently read the account of A.P. Coleman's visit

to Athabasca Pass, and endorsed the professor's conclusion with regard to Mt. Brown, for McEvoy correctly ventured that Mt. Robson was the highest mountain in the Rockies. (Its elevation is 12,972 feet/3954 metres.)

J. Norman Collie and James Outram would, from various summits in 1902, see Mt. Robson out-topping all other peaks on the northwest horizon. But they voiced no immediate desire to make an attempt on it. The first inkling to climb Mt. Robson came about in a most Canadian way. It was a patriotic

---

Opposite: This Byron Harmon photograph, taken in August 1913 during what was probably the third ascent of Resplendent Mountain, is a classic early Canadian mountaineering scene. At first glance it appears to be an archetypal image of five climbers, captured at the pinnacle of the climb. But closer inspection reveals that the climbers are on the way down, and that the first person on the rope (probably Conrad Kain), is facing upslope toward the others. The fourth person on the rope is a child.

Above: George Kinney (l) had fallen from grace, Conrad Kain (c) was about to ascend to prominence, and Curly Phillips (r) had become the premier guide to the northland when Byron Harmon took this photo at Calumet Creek, during the 1911 expedition.

A.P. Coleman's map, showing all that was known of the Mt. Robson region in 1909

act, one of the first initiatives of the Alpine Club of Canada (ACC).

The ACC was formed in 1906, largely at the instigation of surveyor Arthur Oliver Wheeler. As with J.J. McArthur and the other western surveyors of the Dominion Topographic Survey, Wheeler had become a mountaineer when his supervisor assigned him the task of mapping the Selkirk Range of the Columbia Mountains. After his first season in the Selkirks in 1901, Wheeler entertained the idea of forming a Canadian mountaineering club. He discussed the idea with Charles Fay, president of the Appalachian Mountain Club, who was at the time considering the formation of what would become the American Alpine Club. Fay suggested to Wheeler that Canadian mountaineers should

become affiliated with the new American organization. At first Wheeler didn't bite. But after three years of trying to get support from Canadians for an all-Canadian club, he changed his pitch to lobbying for a branch club of the Americans. This brought about a passionate response from an anonymous Winnipeg writer, who took Wheeler to task for being un-Canadian.

The writer was Elizabeth Parker, an employee of the *Winnipeg Free Press*. Enlisting the support of her editor, by early 1906 Parker had written and circulated enough articles to stir public interest for the formation of a Canadian club. What the proponents needed was a venue for the first meeting and a means by which to get its members there. Unlikely as it may seem,

Conrad Kain rounds a serac wall on the south face of Mt. Robson in 1924.

Winnipeg was chosen. At a meeting in February 1906, Wheeler convinced executives of the Canadian Pacific Railway to provide 20 free rail passes for members. The ACC was founded the following month. Wheeler, then aged 45, became its first president.

Wheeler would serve on the ACC executive for 21 years. One of his first suggestions was that, as A.P. Coleman was Canada's most experienced and respected mountaineer, he should make an attempt to climb Mt. Robson as an inaugural activity for the ACC, and before foreigners got to the top of the peak.

Arthur P. Coleman was a professor of Geology and of Natural History at Victoria College at the University of Toronto. A distinguished academic, a talented artist, and a prolific author, Cole-man had travelled extensively. Perhaps recalling the frustrations of his attempts to reach Athabasca Pass in the 1890s, Coleman was not initially flattered by the suggestion that he bash through the woods for the glory of the ACC. But the rumour of Mt. Robson's stature proved too great an attraction, and he soon warmed to the challenge. As was customary, he selected his brother Lucius as a companion. He also asked George Kinney, another accomplished mountaineer, to join the expedition. Kinney was a Methodist minister who had taken to climbing while serving in parishes in Banff and at Field, where he had made the first solo ascent of Mt. Stephen in 1904.

Coleman's first challenge in planning the expedition was deciding how

Conrad Kain leads a roped party near the summit of Mt. Robson in 1924. This was the first time that women climbed the highest peak in the Rockies.

The east face of Mt. Robson in 1911, showing the icy slope of the Kain Face, and the southeast ridge

best to reach Mt. Robson. Although railway survey trails led west from Edmonton, the route was long and plagued with mud and muskeg. Thinking it a shortcut, Coleman chose instead to travel north from Laggan.

The shortcut required almost six weeks – twice as long as planned. Although they were in the vicinity of Mt. Robson for a week, Coleman and his companions never once saw its summit, which was "wrapped in the solitude of centuries." The party tried to climb the impossible-looking south slopes, but a heavy snowfall curtailed the attempt. Coleman and his companions departed in mid-September, hungry, vanquished, but resolved to return.

In late July 1908, the Colemans and Kinney made another attempt. Departing this time from Edmonton, they followed the construction tote road for the Grand Trunk Pacific Railway. In the Athabasca Valley, the party hired Adolphus Moberly to guide them to the north side of Mt. Robson, where Coleman reasoned they would enjoy a greater chance of success because they would be camped at a higher elevation than the previous year.

During their three-week stay, Coleman's party named many features, and made several minor climbs. However, Mt. Robson again eluded them. "Every morning I arose at 3:30 to look at the weather, and then turned in again when the

"In Conrad Kain there was a splendid fire." Of the four 12,000 foot mountains in the Canadian Rockies, Kain was the first (as of 1923) to climb the three highest — Robson, Columbia, and North Twin. It would be fourteen years before another mountaineer did likewise.

George Kinney took this view of Curly Phillips, high on Mt. Robson in 1909.

upper part of Robson was invisible." Only four days were conducive to climbing, and in deference to Reverend Kinney, they spent one of these at rest because it was a Sunday. In their only serious attempt on Mt. Robson, Coleman's party gained the crest of The Dome beneath the east face. Kinney also made a desperate solo attempt on the west face of the mountain – foreshadowing the developments of the following year.

II. THE HIGH WORSHIP OF REVEREND GEORGE KINNEY

BEFORE THE END of the 1908 outing, the Coleman brothers and Kinney made plans to return to Mt. Robson the following summer. However, in May 1909, Kinney heard that "a party of foreigners" was planning an attempt. The mountaineering foreigners were an elite British group – Arnold Mumm (of champagne fame), Geoffrey Hastings (a frequent companion of Collie), Leopold Amery, and Mumm's Swiss guide, Moritz Inderbinen. Each had at least one 20,000-foot summit to his credit. Ironically, although the climbers had designs on Mt. Robson, the ACC planned to treat this British team as royalty. They were to be special guests at the club's annual camp. The clubhouse in Banff was hurried to completion to house them on their arrival.

Making the first ascent of Mt. Robson had become an obsession for Kinney. He could not let the foreigners claim the mountain, nor could he wait

for the Colemans. Leaving his parish duties to his father, he departed alone from Edmonton on June 11 with three horses, three months provisions, and $2.85 in his pocket. Kinney hoped to meet a climbing partner on his way to the mountain. He persuaded the first prospector he met to join the expedition, selling him a horse and half of the provisions. The companion promptly deserted.

Tremendous floods in the Athabasca Valley hampered travel. At one camp Kinney and his supplies became marooned by rising water on one island, while his horses took refuge on another. He eventually moved his camp to John Moberly's

house on the east bank of the river, just downstream from the present location of Jasper. Moberly's dogs ate Kinney's supply of bacon. All Moberly could offer as replacement was a can of lard.

However, fortune was also with Kinney, for at Moberly's house he met Donald "Curly" Phillips, a 25 year-old who was fresh from working on the construction of the Spiral Tunnels near Field. Phillips had been intending to pursue prospecting. Kinney took advantage of Phillips's ignorance of mountaineering and

Where's the champagne? Still dapper after three weeks on the trail: Arnold Mumm (l) and his guide Moritz Inderbinen, in 1910 or 1911.

A.H. MacCarthy leads a roped party descending from Resplendent Mountain in August 1913, a few days after he had participated in the first ascent of Mt. Robson. The climbers are roped too close together. If one had plunged into a crevasse, all probably would have been dragged in.

Three climbers traverse beneath the treacherous serac wall on the south glacier route of Mt. Robson in 1924.

convinced him to join the venture. In all likelihood, Kinney recognized in Phillips a good horseman who could lead him to Mt. Robson.

Phillips later recounted that it wasn't until they had been on the trail for several days that he discovered that Kinney was "a preacher." After that revelation, "I had to lay aside any superfluous language that comes in handy to a fellow driving pack horses or doing other ornery jobs where patience becomes a burden."

Phillips then made another, more ominous discovery for the beginning of a two-month packtrip. "By this time I had got Mr. Kinney's grubstake sized up and could see that we were going to be short of provisions." Kinney was unconcerned. He had brought a rifle to use in supplementing the larder. Near the head of the Moose River, a bull caribou walked into view. Kinney quickly produced the rifle and got off a shot. He missed the caribou, which continue to walk nonchalantly towards them. Phillips took the rifle and fired ten shots at less than fifty yards. All missed. On inspection, Phillips discovered that the rifle barrel was bent, and he silently cursed not having brought his own. Soon after, two more caribou approached. Phillips refrained from the hunt because he "didn't think they'd like to be shot at with a crooked gun."

Kinney and Phillips crossed Robson Pass and made their basecamp near the southwest shore of Berg Lake, close to the starting point for Kinney's intended route on Mt. Robson – the west face. What followed ranks among the more intrepid episodes in the history of Canadian mountaineering. With only a hemp rope, one ice axe, a cane, and a few blankets for equipment, and virtually devoid of rations, the reverend and the greenhorn made four desperate attempts on the treacherous west face of Mt. Robson. These commenced from precarious camps on the mountainside – "High Up," "Higher Up," and "Highest Up." Storms turned back the first three attempts, from which the pair descended to camp and a diet of "birds and marmot."

Kinney's published account of these attempts brims with difficulties, dangers, and the imminence of death. The words ooze self-importance, although he did allow that "Phillips was fast becoming an expert in climbing." It is difficult to say whether Kinney's account was exaggerated. He and Phillips attempted Mt. Robson in appalling weather and under atrocious climbing conditions. They were also forcing a route that was one of the least likely on the mountain. Kinney claimed that their fourth climb, on August 13, typically pursued in the teeth of a storm, brought them the success for which he had been willing to risk so much.

Phillips' later testimony indicated that ice stopped the pair somewhere below the summit. "We reached on our ascent (in mist and storm) an ice-dome fifty or sixty feet high, which we took for the peak. The danger was too great to ascend the dome." The upper part of the Emperor Ridge, which Kinney and Phillips would have had to traverse at the top of the west face, is a kilometre-long, sinuous staircase, covered over by remarkable snow and ice formations called "gargoyles." One mountaineer has since likened these to "a host of white cowled monks."

That Kinney and Phillips made no mention of the gargoyles, nor of the difficulty they would have had in negotiating them, indicates that the pair did not attain that height on the mountain. Kinney recounted poking his cane through a cornice, to reveal a view down the north side of the peak to Berg Lake. This suggests that they gained the crest of the Emperor Ridge at an elevation lower than the gargoyles; possibly as much as 350 m below, and a kilometre distant from the summit. Nonetheless, the courage and the perseverance of Kinney and Phillips were remarkable. To this day, mountaineers generally shun the avalanche-prone west face of Mt. Robson.

After descending a short distance, Kinney left a record of their ascent in a natural cairn. Inside a tin can he stashed a glass vial that contained a note with their names, along with a Canadian flag. In August 1959, a party of American climbers turned back from an attempt on the Emperor Ridge of Mt. Robson. As they descended the upper west face, one climber found the tin can and retrieved its well-preserved contents.

Kinney's claim to the first ascent of Mt. Robson was privately doubted by many in the ACC, particularly by A.O. Wheeler. There were inconsistencies and fabrications in the account of the climb, published in 1910. Kinney also claimed to have been the first white man to have set foot on the mountain, thus snubbing the Coleman brothers and packer John Yates, who had participated in the attempts of 1907 and 1908. (Coleman did not publish his account until 1911.)

As demonstrated by the affair of Collie and Outram, in its early days in Canada, mountaineering was considered a pastime of gentlemen. If a party was unsuccessful on the first attempt of a particular mountain, the peak was considered "earmarked" for those climbers until they returned or bowed out. For Kinney to attempt Mt. Robson without including the Colemans was considered selfish and improper. Kinney's effort was also not "sanctioned" by the ACC – a formality of paramount importance to Wheeler.

It was customary in the mountaineering accounts of the day for authors to downplay difficulties and to shy away from the spotlight. Kinney's account did neither. Its lack of modesty was not in keeping with what was expected of a minister. There was no photographic proof that Kinney and Phillips had reached the summit, and although it was an arrogant assertion by Wheeler, he considered Phillips an unreliable witness because he was not an experienced mountaineer. Wheeler was insistent that the first ascent of Mt. Robson should be a glory claimed by Canadians and by members of the ACC. He could not risk the possibility that Kinney had failed, and that a subsequent attempt by Europeans or Americans would be successful. So he continued to promote an "official" attempt that could be verified.

The controversy added to the disappointment of Kinney. When he had returned from Mt. Robson to Edmonton on September 6, 1909, he had expected a hero's welcome. However, the public and the press were more interested in the arrival of Lord Strathcona, and in the Arctic exploits of Cook and Peary. Kinney went unnoticed.

Kinney's fall from favour was gradual. Typical of the era, it was not discussed publicly. With the exception of a few articles later penned by American mountaineers, there was no further reference to Kinney in mountaineering publications. Late in life, Kinney admitted that he probably had been "mistaken" in his claim to having reached Mt. Robson's summit, but the climbing community continued to black-ball him to his death in 1961; the *Canadian Alpine Journal* did not even carry an obituary.

In contrast, Curly Phillips's reputation was untarnished. He became the most successful outfitter and guide

in Jasper, and had a longstanding and profitable relationship with the ACC. He died in 1930 in an avalanche on Elysium Mountain, northeast of Yellowhead Pass.

Mumm's "party of foreigners" reached Mt. Robson in late August 1909. They attempted the east face, where they narrowly escaped annihilation in an avalanche. In 1910, Mumm and Inderbinen returned, bringing with them J. Norman Collie. Heavy snowfalls in August precluded attempts on Mt. Robson, but the party climbed lesser mountains, including Mumm Peak and Mt. Phillips, and explored north toward the Resthaven Icefield. The same party assembled the following year to explore the remote headwaters of the Smoky River, where they made the first ascent of Mt. Bess. This was Collie's last trip to the Rockies. In 1923, outfitter Fred Stephens wrote to entice the mountaineer to the Canadian wilds again. "Say, friend Norman, come! and let the whole dam[n] world race for dollars." But by then Collie was 64; his career as an explorer was over.

III. For Science and for Sport

In 1910, A.O. Wheeler began organizing a reconnaissance expedition to Mt. Robson that would take to the field the following year. He secured funding from the Canadian, Alberta, and BC governments; the Smithsonian Institution; and the Grand Trunk Pacific Railway. Styled on the Victorian exploits that had pushed the British Empire to remote corners of the world, the goals of the expedition were a curious mix of science and sport. Wheeler picked a talented team, including mountain guide Conrad Kain, and trail guide Donald Phillips. For reasons that no one will ever know, Wheeler also invited George Kinney. The Smithsonian Institution

Arthur O. Wheeler is a perplexing figure in the history of the Rockies. He was the architect of great things, but was also a crusty despot almost universally disliked. This photograph appeared in the 1913 *Canadian Alpine Journal* with the caption: "He who must be obeyed." Wheeler's sense of self-importance often spilled over into arrogance. After making the first ascent of a fine mountain in the Selkirk Range in 1901, he saw to it that the peak be named for himself. No other Canadian surveyor in the west ever did likewise.

contributed scientists – among them its Secretary, Dr. Charles Walcott, the geologist who had discovered the Burgess Shale site near Field.

On the way to and from Mt. Robson, the scientists and guides collected plant and animal species with a zeal and abandon that today would be called plunder. At the expedition camp at Robson Pass, Wheeler marvelled at the mountaineering potential of the area. But with the prospects for a future ACC camp at Robson Pass in mind, he ordered expedition members not to inadvertently ascend any prominent mountains while on their quest for specimens.

This autocratic directive grated upon the mountaineers in the group, especially upon Conrad Kain. The Austrian-born Kain had arrived in the Rockies in 1909. Wheeler observed Kain's considerable talent at the ACC annual camp that year, and subsequently appointed him as the Club's official guide. Kain stole away from the Robson Pass camp one afternoon on the pretence of visiting Emperor Falls. When he returned the following morning, it was after the difficult, solo first ascent of Whitehorn Mountain, the fourth highest peak in the area. Kain left a record of his August 10 ascent in a cairn just below the summit. It

Climbers from the 1913 ACC camp view Mt. Robson from meadows beneath Mumm Peak.

was his 28th birthday.

Wheeler was incensed at Kain's brashness, but the guide justified his risky ascent by saying that he could not bear "being among beautiful mountains and not climbing one." Wheeler believed that Kain had reached the summit, but stated that the ascent could not be "recognized" because it was substantiated only by Kain's "word and [by] that little cairn which may never be seen again." Kain replied: "All right, but I have been to the top and have done what I liked to do."

On another day, Kain and expedition photographer Byron Harmon went for a stroll along Robson Glacier. Kain again courted Wheeler's wrath by stopping only when the pair reached the summit of previously unclimbed Resplendent Mountain, the second highest in the area.

The ACC-Smithsonian Expedition was on the trail for two and a half months. It climbed 30 summits and made the first circuit of Mt. Robson The 1912 report of the expedition consumed 91 pages of the regular volume of the *Canadian Alpine Journal,* plus an additional 97-page special volume. The scientific material of the report was instrumental in establishing Mt. Robson Provincial Park in 1913, BC's second provincial park.

IV. GREATNESS ASSURED

THE 1913 ACC CAMP at Robson Pass was restricted to the attendance of 69 "graduate" mountaineers – those who had "qualified" to join the ACC by having previously climbed a mountain in excess of 10,000 feet. The days of month-long toil over quagmired trails to reach Mt. Robson were gone. The participants journeyed in comfort by train from Edmonton to Mount Robson Siding on the Grand Trunk Pacific Railway, from where Curly Phillips packed their equipment and supplies to the camp.

While most at the camp busied themselves with lesser ascents, Wheeler selected two climbers to accompany Conrad Kain on what everyone hoped would be the first ascent of Mt. Robson. The route that Kain chose for the attempt was one that he had first studied during the 1911 expedition. At that time he had told Wheeler that by ascending Robson Glacier and scaling the icy east face of the mountain, the summit would be reached in eight hours from camp. As events transpired, it was a breezy prediction. The Kain Face, as the route was later named, represented a tremendous leap forward in Canadian mountaineering. Moritz Inderbinen, who had led an attempt on the route in 1909, later told Kain, "I never before saw death so near."

On July 30, Kain guided a party on the second ascent of Resplendent Mountain. He packed with him a blanket to use in a planned bivouac that night. On the way down, he stopped off at treeline alongside Robson Glacier, where he met his clients for the Mt. Robson climb – Albert MacCarthy and William Foster. The trio started at 4:30 AM, ascending the glacier to the east flank of the mountain. Kain, suffering from snow-blindness, tirelessly chopped 600 steps in the steep ice, "as

though inspired." At the top of the face, the party gained the narrow southeast ridge, which they followed to the summit slopes. After great effort and much floundering in deep snow, Kain stepped aside and with customary modesty announced, "Gentlemen, that's as far as I can take you." It was 5:30 PM. They spent fifteen minutes on top, which Kain later described as "ten of pure pleasure and five of teeth chattering."

Not wanting to risk a night exposed at great height, nor a descent of the forbidding east face, Kain led his party down the never-trodden south face of Mt. Robson. Night fell, confining the men to a small ledge at about 10,000 feet. After a restless night, the trio was on the move again at first light, only to discover that Foster and MacCarthy had also developed snow-blindness. Kain returned the party to the camp in Robson Pass two and a half days, and two mountains, after they had left it. Wheeler's jealous desire that Mt. Robson be first climbed by Canadians was fulfilled, although just barely. Whereas all three in the summit party were members of the ACC, only Foster, Deputy Minister of Public Works in BC, was a Canadian. Of him, Wheeler said, "…it does one good to meet a politician who can climb a mountain."

The Kain Face route was not successfully repeated until 1961. The ascent of Mt. Robson was the crowning achievement of Conrad Kain's career, which spanned three decades and included 50 first ascents in Canada, and 30 first ascents in New Zealand. The day after Mt. Robson was first climbed, a party returned from the second ascent of Whitehorn Mountain, bringing with them Kain's record of his 1911 solo ascent, collected from the "little cairn" that Wheeler had predicted "may never be seen again."

"A hard climb on the Extinguisher Tower." A stellar piece of climbing on a crumbling pile of junk. Gravity worked as effectively in 1913 as it does today, yet in the first three decades of climbing in the Rockies, only two climbers perished in falls.

For First Ascents and the Acquisition of Scientific Knowledge

I. THE FRANCHISE OF GERTRUDE BENHAM

MOUNTAINEERING IN THE LATE 19th and early 20th centuries was a patriarchal activity. The shift to a more egalitarian outlook was not gradual. It followed from a series of jolts, the first of which Gertrude Benham delivered in 1904.

By the time the 37 year-old Benham arrived in Canada, she was the veteran of 17 trips to the Alps, where she had tallied 160 climbs. The Rockies were her first stop on a round-the-world mountaineering trip, on which she was spending part of the inheritance left by her father. At Lake Louise, with Hans and Christian Kaufmann as guides, she climbed Mt. Lefroy, Mt. Victoria, Mt. Temple, Mt. Whyte, and Pope's Peak. At Moraine Lake, with Christian as guide, she made the first ascent of Mt. Fay on the day that Charles Fay, for whom the mountain had recently been named, also made an attempt. Hans Kaufmann guided Fay. The Kaufmann brothers may have conspired – Fay's route was a poor one, certain to fail, whereas Benham's was much more likely to succeed. Fay was incensed. He had been

---

Opposite: The province of Alberta entered Confederation in 1905. One of the first details that required sorting out was the delineation of the boundary with British Columbia. It was a monumental job that required 11 seasons of surveying. A.O. Wheeler, president of the Alpine Club of Canada (shown at the camera), picked up the assignment as the BC representative to

the boundary commission. By the time the survey was completed in 1925, Wheeler was 65. He held a tally of summits that probably rivaled that of the most active Swiss guides.

Above: Ed Feuz Jr. inspects the next quarry, Mt. Lyell 3, from the summit of Mt. Lyell 2 in 1926.

In 1914, the Freshfield Glacier was melting back so quickly, this detached ice pinnacle endured while the glacier vanished from view. J.W.A. Hickson and a climbing companion explore the pinnacle for the benefit of photographer Ed Feuz Jr.

allowed to choose the mountain that would commemorate him, and that mountain had been "stolen" by a woman. Fay requested that Peak Six of the Wenkchemna Peaks (now called Mt. Allen) be renamed as a "new" Mt. Fay, so that he might make its first ascent. But Benham bagged that peak, too.

Caring little for wounded male pride, Benham continued her assault on the Rockies with the Kaufmanns, putting up new routes on Mt. Balfour, Mt. Gordon, and Mt. Collie. She was the first woman to climb Mt. Assiniboine. But her most impressive outing in the Rockies was an ascent of Mt. Stephen that began at Lake Louise. With her guides, she left the Chalet at midnight, crossed Abbot Pass, ascended to Duchesnay Pass, and followed the previously unclimbed southeast ridge to Mt. Stephen's summit at 7:00 PM. After downclimbing the hardest part of the peak, the terrific trio caught a few winks on the rocks before descending to Mt. Stephen House at Field, where they woke the staff for an early breakfast.

After leaving the Rockies, Benham climbed in the Selkirks before heading off to New Zealand and Japan. She never returned to Canada but continued her life of adventure into her early seventies. Benham was the first woman to climb Kilimanjaro. She travelled around the world eight times, including four solitary crossings of Africa.

J. Monroe Thorington's party approaches the summit of Mt. Forbes, during its third ascent in 1926.

II. J.W.A. HICKSON: IRON MAN

IT IS NO DISCREDIT to A.P. Coleman to say that he was more an explorer than he was a mountaineer. Although he climbed in wild places, Coleman's ascents were seldom technically difficult. By 1909, Canada had its own mountaineering club, and it had a corps of surveyors who were bagging peaks on the government's tab. What the country lacked was a Canadian of private means who was a mountaineer equal to the guides and the elite climbers from Britain and the United States. Without fanfare, Joseph W.A. Hickson stepped up to fill that void.

After apprenticing for five seasons in the Alps, Hickson made his first climbs in the Rockies in 1909, when he was 36. He would spend 17 summers in the mountains of western Canada, climbing most often with guide Ed Feuz Jr. The pair had a penchant for out-of-the-way places. Their difficult first ascent route on Mt. St. Bride in 1910 was probably not repeated until 1999.

In one of his published articles, Hickson described how he became interested in making an attempt on Cataract Peak in 1930, after noting that he had been erroneously credited with its first ascent in the guidebook to the Rockies. From Devils Thumb near Lake Louise, Hickson and Feuz scoped Cataract Peak and other unclimbed peaks in

Ed Feuz Jr. leads J. Monroe Thorington's party across the bergschrund on Mt. Lyell 3 during its first ascent in 1926. Nobody had been to the Lyell Icefield since James Outram and Christian Kaufmann had climbed Mt. Lyell 2 in 1902. Thorington's party made first ascents of three of the four remaining 11,000-foot Lyell peaks. Peak 3 required three attempts.

Few portraits exist of J. Monroe Thorington in the mountains. He appears on the right in this view taken on the 10,080 foot summit of Mt. Ermatinger in 1928. Thorington's longtime climbing partner, Philadelphia doctor, Max Strummia, is beside him.

its neighbourhood. "Here seemed quite enough material to engage us for a couple of weeks, or longer, if we desired." By the end of that summer – his last spent climbing – Hickson had completed his 31st first ascent in the Rockies. He had also ascended all the 11,000-foot peaks in the Lake Louise district.

Ed Feuz Jr. left this description of Hickson: "If you ever saw him walk down the street, you'd never think he was a mountaineer. He could hardly walk. Years ago a horse he was riding slipped and rolled over his leg and it never healed well. Physically, he was not strong either. But he had an iron will, and he was the most stubborn man I ever met; after all that's what gets you up mountains." J.W.A. Hickson is commemorated by two mountains, one that he climbed in the Rockies, the other in BC's Coast Mountains.

III. Making History:
James Monroe Thorington

James Monroe Thorington was born in 1895, the year after the Yale Lake Louise Club made the first ascent of Mt. Temple. By the time he arrived in the Rockies in 1914, the trails were blazed and the mapping was nearly

completed. Many considered the range to be almost exhausted of challenges. But Thorington would be a pioneer nonetheless, a prolific mountaineer who made 52 first ascents during 15 seasons in western Canada, and who became the greatest historian of the Rockies.

Thorington hailed from Philadelphia As with many American mountaineers of his era, he spent his summers in full-scale expeditions. His most notable exploits in the Rockies were his 1922 journey to the Freshfield Icefield, his 1923 expedition to the Columbia Icefield, his 1924 outing to the headwaters of the Athabasca River, and his 1926 trip to Mt. Lyell and Mt. Forbes. In the space of a week, the 1923 party made the first ascent of North Twin (the third 12,000-foot summit to be climbed in the Rockies), the second ascent of Mt. Columbia, the first ascent of Mt. Saskatchewan, and the third ascent of Mt. Athabasca. As a shortcut from the Alexandra River to the Columbia Icefield, outfitter Jimmy Simpson took the party's horses down the Saskatchewan Glacier.

The mountains in the vicinity of Athabasca Pass held a particular fascination for Thorington. In 1924, his party made the first ascent of the once-fabled Mt. Hooker, and the third ascent of Mt. Brown. Thorington was not convinced that the Hooker-Brown controversy had been properly laid to rest. (He had pursued every thread to exhaustion, even journeying to London with the express purpose of consulting the two, contradictory journals of

Opposite: Trail guide Jimmy Simpson's shortcut from Castleguard Meadows to Sunwapta Pass saved two days on the trail for Thorington's 1923 expedition, but it asked a lot of the horses. On the first passage, it took Simpson most of a day to move the packstring down the Saskatchewan Glacier and over Parker Ridge. But the outing soon became commonplace and remained popular for almost 20 years. This photograph is of interest to glaciologists because it shows a lake on the surface of the glacier, midway between the terminus and the icefield. The lake has long since drained away.

Left: Conrad Kain leads on the first ascent of Mt. Hooker in 1924. A.J. Ostheimer III, then just 16, is one of the other two climbers.

David Douglas.) Thorington speculated that the mountains bearing the names of Hooker and Brown were not those intended by Douglas, and that a goose-chase had been made of a goose-chase. Being well read and evidently possessing a sense of humour, he cited Mark Twain in his argument: "...the researches of many antiquarians have already thrown much darkness on the subject, and it is probable, if they continue, that we shall soon know nothing at all."

A.O. Wheeler, who had officially applied the names of Mt. Brown and Mt. Hooker during the Interprovincial Boundary Survey, and who evidently did not see any humour in the matter, strongly disagreed. He sparred with Thorington in the pages of the *Canadian Alpine Journal.* After stating his case, Thorington let the matter ride, commenting not so much on the historical significance of the quest for the elusive mountains, but on its transformative effect on the participants. "They came from the far corners of the earth, following pioneer trails, seeking beauty. And none there was who returned insensitive to the glory of that mountain vastness."

In the 1920s and early 1930s, Thorington climbed for five seasons with mountain guide, Conrad Kain. After Kain's death in 1934, Thorington edited *Where the Clouds Can Go* – a volume that is part Kain's biography and part his autobiography. Thorington was an inexhaustible writer and compiler, authoring more than 275 titles: bibliographies of historical articles,

Right: Mt. Columbia was the focus of intense interest between 1898 and 1902, but after the first ascent, mountaineers shunned the peak for more than two decades. In this photo, Conrad Kain leads Jimmy Simpson at the summit cornice, on the second ascent in 1923. Simpson had also been trail guide to James Outram's 1902 expedition, but Outram had refused to let him join the climbing team on the first ascent. After topping Mt. Columbia, Simpson resolved to climb it every 21 years. In 1944, Thorington reminded Simpson to make good on the pledge. The crusty trail guide gave a typical reply: "Well, if I'd climbed it in 1902, that would be one thing, but since I didn't do it then, I can't see any reason to do it now."

Opposite: William Ladd and Conrad Kain take a break before tackling the final tier of cliffs on lofty Mt. Saskatchewan, during the first ascent in 1923.

toponomies, lists of routes, and descriptions of mountain passes. He co-edited the first six editions of *A Climber's Guide to the Rocky Mountains of Canada*, which for 70 years was the only alpine climbing guidebook for the range. He noted the centennial of the first ascent of Mt. Brown, and the centennial of Sir George Simpson's crossing of Athabasca Pass, and he wrote articles commemorating these events. He edited the American Alpine Club's journal and served as that club's president. An ophthalmologist by profession, Thorington's output in the medical literature was no less impressive.

Collie and Stutfield, Coleman, Wilcox, Outram, and Thorington each wrote classic books about the early exploration of the Rockies. Thorington's 1925 work, *The Glittering Mountains of Canada*, is the finest for its story of exploration and for its grasp of history: "...for here is Geography in the making, and with a tradition behind it – a story that has never been properly gathered together, and whose details, in part at least, are gone forever."

It seems that few of the old-time mountaineers died young. But even in longevity Thorington excelled. He passed away in 1989, outliving all of his contemporaries.

IV. W.O. FIELD: A CAREER MOVE

THIRTY YEARS AFTER the Yale Lake Louise Club climbed the peaks and toured the valleys around Lake Louise, schoolmates from another prestigious institu-

tion – Harvard – teamed to explore the Rockies. The 1924 outing was organized by 20-year-old William Osgood Field, who would, after graduating, establish a career as the preeminent expert on glaciers of the northern hemisphere.

Field began his acquaintance with glaciers on the trail north from Lake Louise. Members of the party, led by guides Joseph Biner and Ed Feuz Jr., made the first ascents of Mt. Patterson, Epaulette Mountain, Mt. Outram, and South Twin. At the Columbia Icefield, they also climbed North Twin (second ascent) and Castleguard Mountain. Among other things, the expedition was notable for its photography. Several of the climbers carried small cameras, creating part of the legacy of some 7000 images now housed in the W.O.

Field collection at the Archives and Library of the Whyte Museum in Banff. W.O. Field's notebooks, crammed with glacier observations, also reside there. Field's love of the ice rivers of western Canada and Alaska was lifelong. He made his last working trip to the mountains at age 77, and lived to be 90.

V. A.J. Ostheimer's Not Bad Summer

"The weather bureaus had forecasted a bad summer; we decided, at a meeting of the outfit the night before starting, that we would not have a bad summer. And thus we commenced our work." It was to be a labour the likes of which had not been seen before in the Canadian Rockies, nor has it been

W.O. Field's party traverses beneath the summit of Castleguard Mountain at the Columbia Icefield, in 1924.

seen since. In a period of 64 days spent at the headwaters of the Whirlpool, Athabasca, and Wood rivers, the 1927 expedition of Alfred James Ostheimer III climbed 36 mountains, 27 of which were first ascents.

Mountaineering in the Rockies had come a long way in the century since David Douglas's climb of Mt. Brown. Everyone on the 1927 expedition climbed: cooks, guides, and packers. Ostheimer, a student at Harvard, was 19 at the time, but was no fledgling mountaineer. He had been to the Rockies with Thorington in 1924 and 1926, when, among other peaks, he had climbed Mt.

Hooker and four of the summits of Mt. Lyell. He had also topped Mt. Temple in the Rockies, and Mt. Rainier – highest of the North Cascades.

One leg of the 1927 outing epitomized the party's intensity and focus. Just after midnight on July 2, Ostheimer and guide Hans Fuhrer ascended the Columbia Glacier, hoping to make the third ascent of North Twin – third highest in the Rockies. After waiting out a blizzard, they groped through fog to the summit of North Twin at 6:00 PM. From there they headed east to the summit of Stutfield Peak, then south and east in the dark to Mt. Kitchener

After the trials of the ascent to Epaulette Mountain's summit, W.O. Field's party savoured the view of the mighty trio of the Mistaya Valley – (l-r) Mt. Chephren, White Pyramid, and Howse Peak.

(both were first ascents), south to Snow Dome (a second ascent), and then – declining to attempt Mt. Columbia because of wretched weather and a shortage of food – back down the tottering, serac-filled chaos of Columbia Glacier, hallucinating all the way to camp. In 36 hours they had travelled 61 kilometres.

The accomplishments of Ostheimer's expedition are even more remarkable given the weather of 1927. The forecasters were correct. It was no blissful summer, but a fickle mix of storm and chill that would deter most modern climbers.

Although the primary focus in 1927 was mountaineering, Ostheimer justified his claim that the expedition was "for first ascents and the acquisition of scientific knowledge," by penning an 11-page article that described the flora and fauna observed on the trip. In his journals, Ostheimer also recorded detailed descriptions of fossils, glaciers, and geology. As was the case with several other mountaineers of note in the Rockies, Ostheimer virtually ceased to climb after his extraordinary summer. He became a successful businessman, selling, of all things, life insurance.

Although 23 years had passed since Jean Habel first visited the upper Athabasca Valley, the rigors of trail life had changed little for members of W.O. Field's 1924 expedition.

Epilogue

As the footfalls of A.J. Ostheimer's 1927 expedition faded from the Athabasca Valley, so did the late-Victorian holdover of "climbing for knowledge." For the majority of future mountaineers in the Rockies, climbing would be purely a sport of leisure and challenge. And, despite Hugh Stutfield's assessment of 1902, that the mountaineering possibilities of the range were all but exhausted, there would be many challenges.

At first, climbers turned their attention to summits that were technically difficult by any route – mountains such as Mt. Alberta and Brussels Peak. Then came the notion of forcing more and more difficult lines on familiar mountains, first in summer, then in winter – the north faces of Mt. Edith Cavell and Mt. Temple. Some mountaineers undertook mini-traverses, such as along the crest of the Wenkchemna Peaks, or they connected icefields into marathon ski routes through the heart of the Rockies. A smattering of far-flung peaks continued to entice climbers into the wilds – Mt. Harrison, the last 11,000 footer to be climbed, didn't see an ascent until 1964. In the late 1960s and the early 1970s, Canadians pushed the frontiers of waterfall ice climbing. Finally came alpine routes in the 1980s and 1990s that put many of these aspects together – winter ascents of Mt. Fay, Mt. Bryce, Mt. Goodsir South, Mt. Chephren, and Howse Peak – each among the more difficult and dangerous climbs in the world.

But in all the travelling to and from these mountains, most who followed in the footsteps of the early mountaineers were unaware of the stories of those who climbed a century ago. No matter. Bush, rock, and river are great equalizers; the Rockies have a way of delivering understanding. Even close to a highway, mountaineers can still stumble into pockets of wilderness that negate the advantages of modern equipment, and arrest the passing of time. Adventure awaits. With a little imagination, a mountaineer stumped today by a canyon on the approach to a peak might hear the ghostly echoes of broadaxe from a nearby tangle of pines, the cursing of packers as they coaxed the string along a precipice above the river, and the campfire conversations where the climbs of tomorrow were created, and the climbs of yesterday re-lived. J. Monroe Thorington knew this magic of the mountains when he wrote in 1925: "We were not pioneers ourselves, but we journeyed over old trails that were new to us, and with hearts open. Who shall distinguish?"

Author's Notes

Many people consider the Canadian Rockies to be any mountains in Alberta and BC. Properly speaking, the Rockies are the first ranges of mountains when approached from the east. The Columbia Mountains are next (including the Purcell, Selkirk, and Monashee ranges), followed by the northern Cascade Mountains, and the Coast Mountains. Although several of the mountaineers mentioned in this book contributed significantly to exploration of the Columbia Mountains, I have restricted this history to accounts from the Rockies.

When referring to the railway station at Lake Louise, I have retained the name Laggan, which was used until 1913. I have used "Lake Louise" to refer to the lake and its surroundings.

I have used Imperial measurement for elevations of mountains. Although tough climbs can be had on peaks of any elevation, the benchmark for "serious" alpine mountaineering in the Rockies is 11,000 feet. Fifty-four peaks exceed this elevation; four of these exceed 12,000 feet. Of peaks between 10,000 feet and 11,000 feet in elevation ("10,000 footers"), there are approximately 500, of which 314 are named.

Here are useful Imperial/Metric equivalents:
3.281 feet = 1 metre
10,000 feet = 3048 metres
11,000 feet = 3353 metres
12,000 feet = 3657 metres.

The Author

Graeme Pole has climbed more than 250 summits in the Rockies, some greater, mostly lesser. As with many of the mountaineers described in these pages, he favours out-of-the-way places. Graeme lives with his family near Hazelton in northwestern BC, where he serves as a paramedic. This is his eighth book. Visit his website: www.mountainvision.ca

Author photo: Doug McConnery

Acknowledgments

I conducted much of my research at the Archives and Library of the Whyte Museum of the Canadian Rockies, in Banff. Don Bourdon, Head Archivist; Lena Goon, Archives Assistant; and Elizabeth Kundert-Cameron, Librarian; were patient and helpful with my many requests for documents, photographs, and information. Don, in particular, was most accommodating to this project. Other archivists who provided assistance were Jim Bowman and Pat Molesky at the Glenbow Museum Archives; Kelly-Ann Nolin at the BC Archives; Meghan Power at the Jasper Archives; Kate Miller and Rachael Swann at the Alpine Club Library in London; and Jill Delaney at the National Archives in Ottawa. Martha Moore at the Appalachian Mountain Club Archives, and Bridget Burke at the Henry S. Hall Jr. Library of the American Alpine Club, rooted through their holdings to produce archival gold. My deepest thanks go to both. Doug McConnery kindly boxed up his set of the Canadian Alpine Journal and shipped it by bus, allowing me to consult at home material that would otherwise have required another expedition from the backwoods of BC. I am grateful to Rick Collier, Dave Cottingham, John Martin, Bob Saunders, and Don Zerke for research assists. Mike Henderson, Nadine Delorme, Diane McIvor, and Mike McIvor housed and fed me during my research trip to Banff. Marnie Pole and Dave Cottingham provided invaluable commentary on the first draft of the manuscript. As always, I am grateful to Stephen Hutchings for his ambition as a publisher, and to the rest of the team at Altitude.

Bibliography

The information in this book was drawn from more than 200 sources. Many of the contemporary accounts appeared in: the (British) *Alpine Journal*, the *American Alpine Journal*, *Appalachia*, the *Canadian Alpine Journal*, and *The Geographical Journal*. The Annual Reports of the Department of the Interior provided information on the activities of the Dominion Topographic Survey.

Boles, Glen W., William L. Putnam, and Roger W. Laurilla. *Placenames of the Canadian Alps*. Revelstoke: Footprint Publishing, 1990.

Cavell, Edward. *Legacy in Ice*. Banff: The Whyte Foundation, no date.

Coleman, Arthur P. *The Canadian Rockies, New and Old Trails*. Toronto: Henry Frowde, 1911.

Collie, John Norman. *Climbing on the Himalaya and Other Mountain Ranges*. Edinburgh: David Douglas, 1902.

Fay, Charles. *Alpina Americana, Number 2*. New York: American Alpine Club, 1911.

Hart. E.J. *Diamond Hitch*. Banff: Summerthought, 1979.

Kain, Conrad and J. Monroe Thorington. *Where the Clouds Can Go*. New York: American Alpine Club, 3rd ed., 1979.

Kaufmann, Andrew J., and William L. Putnam. *The Guiding Spirit*. Revelstoke: Footprint Publishing, 1986.

Mill, Christine. *Norman Collie, A Life in Two Worlds*. Aberdeen: Aberdeen University Press, 1987.

Ostheimer, A.J. *Every Other Day*. Canmore: Alpine Club of Canada, 2002. R.W. Sandford and Jon Whelan, editors.

Outram, James. *In the Heart of the Canadian Rockies*. New York: The Macmillan Company, 1905.

Sandford, R.W. *The Canadian Alps, Volume I*. Banff: Altitude Publishing, 1990.

Sandford, R.W. *The Guiding Spirit*. Canmore: Alpine Club of Canada & Canadian Pacific Hotels, 1999.

Scott, Chic. *Pushing the Limits*. Calgary: Rocky Mountain Books, 2000.

Smith, Cyndi. *Off the Beaten Track*. Jasper: Coyote Books, 1989.

Stutfield, Hugh E.M. and J. Norman Collie. *Climbs and Exploration in the Canadian Rockies*. London: Longmans, Green and Co., 1903.

Taylor, William C. *The Snows of Yesteryear*. Toronto: Holt, Rinehart and Winston of Canada Ltd., 1973.

Thorington, J. Monroe and William Lowell Putnam. *A Climber's Guide to the Rocky Mountains of Canada*. New York: American Alpine Club, 6th ed., 1966.

Thorington, J. Monroe. *The Glittering Mountains of Canada*. Philadelphia: John W. Lea, 1925.

Unsworth, Walt. *Encyclopedia of Mountaineering*. Hammondsworth: Penguin Books Ltd., 1977.

Whyte, Jon and Carole Harmon. *Lake Louise, A Diamond in the Wilderness*. Banff: Altitude Publishing, 1982.

Wilcox, Walter D. *The Rockies of Canada*. New York: G.P. Putnam's and Sons, 1909.

The Photographs

In the early days, mountaineers generally only brought out their cameras during halts. It wasn't until the 1930s that the skill of the mountaineering photographers, and the equipment that they used in each discipline, attained a convergence that permitted "action shots." As a result, there exist more early photographs of climbers eating breakfasts or posing on summits than there do of climbers grappling with cliffs and icefalls.

Individual photographers are credited where known.

Alpine Club Library, London
54, Hugh Stutfield (001070GL)

Appalachian Mountain Club Archives, Boston
28 (59-21); 33 (59-73)

British Columbia Archives, Victoria
91 (F-05684)

Glenbow Museum Archives, Calgary
60 right (NA-699-1); 66, J.N. Collie (NA-3551-89); 67, Jack Robson (NA-3551-14); 68, J.N. Collie (NA-3551-60); 69, Jack Robson (NA-3551-80); 70 (NA-3551-62); 71 (NA-3551-53); 83 top, Byron Harmon (NA-2696-4); 85 lower (NA-1644-1); back cover, Byron Harmon (NA-2696-4)

Henry S. Hall Jr. American Alpine Club Library, and Colorado Mountain Club Collection
J. Monroe Thorington Collection, scrapbook titled "Expedition to the Forbes-Lyell Group, Rocky Mountains of Canada, 1926": 95; 97; 98

National Archives of Canada, Ottawa
8 (PA 23141); 11 lower (PA-042179); 15 (NMC 009877); 41 (PA-099822)

Collection of Graeme Pole
2, Cyril G. Wates; 10-11, W.S. Drewry; 12, J.J. McArthur; 13; 16, W.D. Wilcox; 24, J.H. Scattergood; 25, P.D. McTavish; 27, Detroit Photographic Co.; 34-35, Byron Harmon; 35 lower; 36; 37, J.H. Scattergood; 42, A.P. Coleman; 43, J.N. Collie; 46, W.D. Wilcox; 48, Jean Habel; 55; 58, Francklyn; 60 left, James Outram; 64, James Outram; 74; 80; 87, J.M. Thorington; 90, Julia Henshaw; 100, 101, 102, 103, J.M. Thorington (all four); 105, W.O. Field

Provincial Archives of Alberta, Edmonton
94 (A-10-726)

Whyte Museum of the Canadian Rockies, Banff
front cover (V364/36 LC); 5, W.O. Field, (V6 66 O/S); 6 (V6/PD3, p. 43); 9, J.J. McArthur (*Appalachia* Vol. VIII, opp. p. 1); 10 lower (03.7 D49); 14, J.J. McArthur (*Appalachia* Vol. VII, opp. p. 26); 17 (V396/PA 4); 18 (02.6 W54); 19 (02.6 Se 4g); 20 top, W.D. Wilcox (NA 66-551); 20 lower, W.D. Wilcox (NA 66-2251); 21, S.E.S. Allen (NA 66-734); 22-23 (V527 PS-IIIA-114); 23 lower (M88/309); 26 (V321/PA-16); 29, Herschel C. Parker (V 321/PA-76); 30, Herschel C. Parker (V 321/PA-21); 31 top (V14 AC 33P/119, p. 38); 31 lower (NA 66-1283); 32 (V22 p. 33); 38 (V653/NA 80-1130); 39 (NA 80-1406); 40 (NA 80 328); 47 (V622 NA-3); 49 (V62 NA 66-1248); 50-51 (V364/117 PA); 53, Mary Schäffer (V439 PS-20); 56, J.N. Collie (V497/PA 51-88a); 59, Edward Whymper (NA 66-2270); 61, Edward Whymper (V728/NA 66-2274); 62 (V321/PA-79); 63, James Outram (*Appalachia* Vol. X, opp. p. 48); 65, James Outram (*Appalachia* Vol. X, opp. p. 48); 72, Hermann Woolley (V14-AC-OP-57); 73 (V14/AC-OOP-151); 75 (NA 66-1189); 77 (V364/36 LC); 78, Byron Harmon (NA 71-936); 79 (V263/NA71-1148); 81, H. Pollard (V14/AC 192 P 1-153); 82, H. Pollard (V14/AC 192P 1-155); 83 lower, Byron Harmon (V622 PA 128-10); 84-85, George Kinney (NA 66-508); 86 (V14/AC 33P 116-79); 93, P.L. Tait (V14/AC 33P 116-62); 96, E. Feuz Jr. (V200/PA 44-94); 99 (V622/PA 128-15); 104 (V200/PA 44-40); 106 (V6/145PA F-48-R-59)